This book belongs to

Ayana

It's a GOOD
MORNING
Just Because
YOU LOVE
ME

BroadStreet
P U B L I S H I N G

BroadStreet Publishing Group LLC
Racine, Wisconsin, USA
Broadstreetpublishing.com

It's a Good Morning Just Because You Love Me

© 2016 by BroadStreet Publishing

ISBN 978-1-4245-5197-2 (hard cover)
ISBN 978-1-4245-5224-5 (e-book)

Devotional entries composed by Diane Dahlen, Cari Dugan, Laura Krause, Shannon Lindsay, Cate Mezyk, and Stephanie Sample.

Design by Chris Garborg | garborgdesign.com
Edited and compiled by Michelle Winger | literallyprecise.com

Printed in China.

16 17 18 19 20 21 22   7 6 5 4 3 2 1

The LORD is merciful
and compassionate,
slow to get angry and filled
with unfailing love.
The LORD is good to everyone.
He showers compassion
on all his creation.

PSALM 145:8-9 NLT

Introduction

Choose to believe that today will be a good day!

Life challenges can quickly drain us of our strength. For those who have put their hope in the Lord, there is a constant source of refreshing.

Let these scriptures, devotions, and prayers encourage you to spend time with God each day. Delight in the promises found in his Word, and discover the joy of his presence. Let the knowledge of his unfailing love renew your strength and put a smile on your face.

Because God loves you, it really is a good morning!

JANUARY

Blessed is the one you choose and bring near,

to dwell in your courts!

We shall be satisfied with the goodness

of your house,

the holiness of your temple!

PSALM 65:4 ESV

Fresh and New

Therefore, if anyone is in Christ, the new creation has come:
The old has gone, the new is here!
2 CORINTHIANS 5:17 NIV

When we accept Christ as our Savior, we get to start over, as if from
scratch. Our old, ugly lives and selfish ways are forgotten, and we
are brand new. Oh goodness, aren't you thankful for it? We all have
plenty of days we could happily erase: memories of bad choices we
made and poor decisions followed through.

Every day, we get to stand before our King and hold our heads up
high, knowing we are forgiven and clean. There's no checklist of our
sins and faults, no remembering the worst of our mistakes. Instead,
there is the tender love of our Father's heart, flowing down in
abundance upon us, making us new.

Lord, I'm once again in awe of the depth of your love for me.
Thank you for the gift of forgiveness and for making me fresh
and new.

JUST PRAY

Then he prays to God, and is accepted by him,
he comes into his presence with joy,
and God repays him for his righteousness.

JOB 33:26 NRSV

It's easy to become overwhelmed by expectations. We want to fit in, to belong, but the formula is constantly changing, and it's hard to know whose standards we should shoot for: family, work, friends, society, social media...who decides what's acceptable?

Look carefully at the verse. What must we do in order to be accepted by God? Must we have our acts together, our sinful habits conquered, our church attendance perfect? No. Just pray. We pray to God, and he welcomes us in. Scrubbed and shiny or worse for wear, it's all the same to him. He sees you, he hears you, and he invites you into his joyful presence.

Father, help me to remember yours is the standard of acceptance that matters most, and that just by praying I've already met it. Thank you for loving me as I am.

SHOW ME YOUR GLORY

So the LORD said to Moses, "I will also do this thing that you have spoken; for you have found grace in My sight, and I know you by name," And he said, "Please, show me Your glory."

EXODUS 33:17–18 NKJV

The sky is gray. Rain is falling, and your hair is just not happening. Last night's dishes clutter the sink, and a mountain of mail covers the counter. Everywhere you look, beauty seems to be taking a break.

Close your eyes. Say his name. *Jesus.* Now open them, and look again. See that little spot of blue sky, that single ray of light sneaking through the clouds? Notice the water drops resting on the hostas. Remember the tasty meal that created the mess. The mail may still be jumbled, and your hair may still be doing its own thing, but beauty is here, always, just one sweet word away. *Jesus.* Let his glory inform your sight.

Lord, when I focus on you, when I say your name, I can't help but see beauty all around me. Thank you for the surprise and delight of discovering beauty in unexpected places.

THE GIVER OF GOOD GIFTS

Every good thing given and every perfect gift is from above, coming down from the Father of lights, with whom there is no variation or shifting shadow.

JAMES 1:17 NASB

Count your blessings. It's become a phrase we throw around so often, it may have lost its meaning. But seriously, have you ever done it? Where do we begin? According to this verse in the book of James, every good thing in our lives is a blessing. Every good thing. Ready? Go.

Maybe today is "one of those days," and you're having trouble getting started. Your home, work, and social life all seem more like burdens than blessings. It's okay. Just begin here, with the greatest blessing of them all:

Father, you are the giver of good gifts. Even on the days I can't see any good, I can still see you. I always have my Father in heaven, unchanging, sending down blessings like rays of light.

ASK ANYTHING

This is the confidence we have in approaching God: that if we ask anything according to his will, he hears us. And if we know that he hears us—whatever we ask—we know that we have what we asked of him.

1 JOHN 5:14-15 NIV

Think of a time you wanted something, maybe from a parent or your boss, but you were afraid to ask. Why were you afraid? Perhaps you feared you didn't deserve it. Or possibly, you wanted it, but you also knew it wasn't necessarily good for you. Whether you're an adult asking for a day off work or a teenager asking for permission to stretch a curfew, it can be difficult to ask boldly for what you want, especially if you're not entirely certain you should have it.

Take heart in these words from 1 John, and know that when you place your relationship with God as your top priority, you can ask him for anything. Anything! When we most desire to be in his will, he gladly grants our other requests.

God, you are my deepest desire. Knowing I can come to you with my needs, my dreams, and my unspoken longings brings comfort to my soul. Boldly, I lay my requests at your feet. I know the answer will be just what I need.

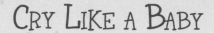

CRY LIKE A BABY

As one whom his mother comforts,
so I will comfort you;
you shall be comforted in Jerusalem.
You shall see, and your heart shall rejoice.
ISAIAH 66:13–14 ESV

Few images are more peaceful than that of a mother sweetly comforting her child. Imagine the tenderness of her embrace and the gentleness of her voice. This is the picture God gave Isaiah to explain how he comforts us when we let him. So let him. Give up the struggle, and let him.

It's okay to cry like a baby. It's okay to just close your eyes and snuggle into his arms. He wants you there! Listen to the sound of his voice; listen to how much he loves you. Fall in with his gentle sway, and let him fill you with his joy.

Father, I need you. I need you to hold me and love me and tell me everything's going to be okay. Help me settle into your embrace, to stop struggling. Whisper in my ear, "I've got you, dear one. I've got you."

A SAFE PLACE

My God is my rock.
I can run to him for safety.
He is my shield and my saving strength,
my defender and my place of safety.
The LORD saves me from those who want to harm me.

2 SAMUEL 22:3 NCV

In some seasons of life, the attacks seem to come from all sides. Just as we find shelter from the arrows in the east, the spears arrive from the north. When the Old Testament was written, these battles were literal: the arrows were actual arrows.

Today, the arrows look more like bank statements, work pressures, and ailing parents, but our source of refuge is the very same. God is your safe place. When you run to him, he is always there; he will defend, protect, and deliver you from whatever you face. His deliverance may not look like you imagine, but if you trust him, it will come.

My God, you are my rock. You are my safety, my best defense, and my only salvation. I stand on your promise, I rest in your love, and I wait for your deliverance.

WONDERFUL COUNSELOR

You make known to me the path of life;
in your presence there is fullness of joy;
at your right hand are pleasures forevermore.

PSALM 16:11 ESV

In high school, we wonder what to do with our lives—what college to attend, what area of study to pursue, and even which of our friendships are building us up. The guidance counselor is just down the hall. The door is usually open and advice is wisely dispensed. We leave feeling lighter, more certain about our next move. The process is pretty simple.

Jesus gives us the Holy Spirit, a wonderful counselor. When we take our questions to him, he not only shines the light on our next steps, he does something more: he fills us with joy. When the Lord guides the way, we move confidently, joyfully, from one place of promise to the next.

Holy Spirit, be my guide. I choose to walk with you; I trust the path you have for me to travel, and I eagerly await the fullness of your joy.

LIFETIME GUARANTEE

I would have despaired unless I had believed that I would see
the goodness of the LORD In the land of the living.
Wait for the LORD;
Be strong and let your heart take courage;
Yes, wait for the LORD.
PSALM 27:13-14 NASB

Would you give your heart to someone you knew would break it, or
accept a job you knew you'd be fired from? Probably not. Faced with
a grave illness, you wouldn't undergo a treatment that was certain
to fail. It's hope that invites us to commit. We aren't guaranteed an
unbroken heart, a 40-year career, or a full recovery, but because it's
possible, we move forward.

There is one promise, one guarantee we can hang our very lives on.
God is good. He wants good for us, and if we hope in him, we will
have it. Grab onto this promise. Believe it, and wait for him to
fulfill it.

Lord, I believe you. I place my hope in you, and I will wait—all
my life—for you. Your promises are true, your word is my
courage, and your love is my strength.

TWIRLING WITH JOY

You changed my sorrow into dancing.
You took away my clothes of sadness,
and clothed me in happiness.
I will sing to you and not be silent.
LORD, my God, I will praise you forever.
PSALM 30:11-12 NCV

Abandoned, abused single mother finds true love, purpose, and healing. That's a movie most of us would watch. Who doesn't love a good restoration story? When God heals broken places and redeems lost situations, our hearts swell with possibility. If he can restore her life, he can surely come in and fix mine.

It's true. The mourners will dance, clothed in happiness. Voices silenced by sadness will sing loudest songs of praise. And you, regardless of what you face today, will be there. Twirling with joy, singing your heart out, you will be there.

Lord, like a dancer spinning with grace, you turn things around. You restore what is broken and redeem what is lost. I praise you for your goodness. Hear my voice, delight in my dance—it is all for you.

Truly Awesome

By the word of the Lord the heavens were made,
their starry host by the breath of his mouth.
He gathers the waters of the sea into jars;
he puts the deep into storehouses.

PSALM 33:6-7 NIV

"These cookies are awesome!"
"Wow, you look awesome today!"
The word *awesome* has slipped into American speech so thoroughly, we may have lost sight of its true meaning. The cookies, though delicious, probably don't inspire overwhelming reverence. Your friend looks gorgeous, but you're not truly taken aback, knocked to your knees.

Only God does that. Reread the Scripture above out loud, lingering over its meaning. Ponder all he has done and will do. This is God; this is your Father! He can hold an ocean in his hand, and yet he knows every hair on your head. He lovingly anticipates every move you make. He delights in *you*, and that is truly awesome.

Lord God, I am in awe of you. When I consider the universe, formed by your breath, and the oceans as merely jars in your storehouse, I can barely contain my amazement. And the fact that you love me—in all my imperfection—is more than I can fathom. Truly, you alone are worthy of my praise.

ONLY FOR YOU

No king is saved by the multitude of an army;
A mighty man is not delivered by great strength.
A horse is a vain hope for safety;
Neither shall it deliver any by its great strength.
Behold, the eye of the Lord is on those who fear Him,
On those who hope in His mercy.

PSALM 33:16-18 NKJV

Some of the most beautiful voices will never be heard on the radio.
Many truly brilliant athletes will never compete at the highest level,
and countless gifted business people will launch companies that fail.
Giftedness, preparation, and resources are no guarantee of our plans
succeeding. And when they don't, we can't help but ask, "God, you
made me great at this, so where is my success?"

The people behind us, our abilities, and our resources aren't the key.
Only God decides if, when, and how we succeed, and it may not look
a thing like we imagined. When things that "should" work out, don't
work out, it's time to shift our perspective—to his. Maybe your voice is
meant just for him, or to be a blessing and comfort to someone close
to you. Your athletic ability may be leading you to coaching. Success
and its measure are decided by God alone.

God, I thank you for the gifts you have given me, and I
surrender them to you. I will measure my success not in
worldly terms, but by the pleasure I feel from you. I will run,
sing, dance, and dream only for you.

COME, AND BE HEALED

For with you is the fountain of life;
in your light we see light.
    PSALM 36:9 NRSV

When you're thirsty, do you run to the desert or the fountain? Stumbling in the darkness, do you fumble for the light, or squeeze your eyes shut? In need of comfort, we seek out relief. In need of illumination, we seek the light.

God is both; he is all. He is the fountain for our thirst, the light for our path. The Lord satisfies our hunger, answers our questions, and heals our hurts. All we have to do, the one necessary thing, is to come to him. He can only quench us if we drink of him. In order to see light, we must enter it. Open your mouth; drink deeply. Open your eyes and see. Come into his presence and be healed.

Father, I've been wandering in this desert for so long, my eyes squeezed tightly against the blowing, drifting sands. Draw me into your presence! I lay my needs, my questions, and my doubts at your feet. Eyes wide open, I bathe in your light.

ALL COMFORT

All praise to God, the Father of our Lord Jesus Christ. God is our merciful Father and the source of all comfort. He comforts us in all our troubles so that we can comfort others. When they are troubled, we will be able to give them the same comfort God has given us. For the more we suffer for Christ, the more God will shower us with his comfort through Christ.

2 CORINTHIANS 1:3-5 NLT

There are many things in this world we tend to look to for comfort. Sometimes it might be food, a hot shower, an air-conditioned room, family, friends, television, a good book...the list is endless.

The Word of God says our merciful Father is the source of all comfort. His promise is to comfort us in all of our troubles. How often do we look elsewhere for comfort when our true comforter is the one who created us and knows our every need?

Oh Father, I pray that today I would look to you to be my source of all comfort. I pray you would teach me to receive my comfort from you and in turn be a comfort to others.

BEYOND YOUR SIGHT

From the end of the earth I call to you
when my heart is faint.
Lead me to the rock
that is higher than I.
PSALM 61:2 ESV

Have you ever wandered through a maze? Even though you may be good at solving mazes on paper, moving through shrubbery or stalks of corn at ground level, you are bound to run into a dead end or two. If only there were a place to climb up high, and see the way through. So what can you do? Call for help; follow the voice of someone who can see more than you.

When life feels like a maze, and you're faint from the exhaustion of running into walls, call out to God. Follow the sound of his voice to the next turn. Allow his hand to lift you up—beyond your own sight—and show you the way through. He is there, listening, waiting to guide you through.

Lord, how wonderful it is to know that when I am lost, I can call to you. Your voice will be my beacon and your hand will lift me up. You show me what otherwise can't be seen, and for this I thank you and praise you.

I WANT TO YEARN

O God, you are my God; I seek you,
my soul thirsts for you;
my flesh faints for you,
as in a dry and weary land where there is no water.
PSALM 63:1 NRSV

What is your deepest, truest desire? Is there something—or someone—
you'd wander through the desert for? Few of us can honestly say we
yearn for God with the marrow-deep longing of King David, but don't
let this verse shame you into believing you are not "spiritual enough."
More likely, we don't share the desperation simply because we've
never enjoyed the same intimacy the "man after God's own heart"
had with him.

Rather than feeling guilty for not equaling David's passion, let us see
this verse as an invitation, as a glimpse into the depth of relationship
that's possible with our Father. Just imagine the communion and the
pure joy that inspired such a desperate cry for his presence. Ask him
for a taste.

Lord, I know that the longings of my heart can never compare
to the glory of knowing you intimately. I want to want you like
King David, Father! Take away my earthly yearnings, and fill
me with desire for only you.

BETTER THAN LIFE

Your unfailing love is better than life itself;
how I praise you!
   PSALM 63:3 NLT

We've all heard about the dessert, or the necklace, or the dress that was "to die for." What is meant, of course, is delicious, beautiful, a perfect fit. As brownies, baubles, and body-flattering clothes go, they are the pinnacle. Clearly, a girl's not about to throw herself in front of a moving train to get her hands on the perfect little black dress. Only one thing is truly better than life, and that's life with the Maker.

Do we believe this? *Can* we believe it this side of heaven? It's easier on the days when life's not so great, but even when things are going our way, even when life couldn't be better, how great is God's promise that what awaits us is *so much better* than anything we can ask or imagine here on earth! His love never fails, and nothing compares. Regardless of the season we are in or the day we are having, let's acknowledge this beautiful truth from his Word.

Lord, nothing compares to your love. On my worst day, I find comfort in your promise. On my best, I marvel at the knowledge that so much more awaits me in heaven. You are bigger than life, you are better than life, and you are the love of my life. How I praise you. Oh, how I love you.

MAKE MY DAY

Fill us with your love every morning.
Then we will sing and rejoice all our lives.

PSALM 90:14 NCV

Seek him first. Why is this such a recurring suggestion, both in the Bible and among followers of Christ? If you regularly begin your days with the Lord, you already know what a day-maker he is. If you haven't settled into the practice, start tomorrow. See how his loving presence affects your days.

Before the day has a chance to disappoint you, before the enemy finds a way to distract you, seek him first. Invite him into every waking moment. Sense him in your interactions and your transactions. Notice the tenderness with which he sees the people you encounter. Invite him to contribute to your decisions. Observe how he consistently places you on the path of love. Allow him to carry your burdens, and see if a joyful song doesn't swell inside you. Allow it to overtake your heart.

Jesus, I invite you to make my day. Let my words, my thoughts, and my actions be yours. Replace my irritations and frustrations with your patience and compassion. Fill me with your love, that all I do may reflect it onto others. Fill my heart with your song, that I may sing it over all who can hear.

His

Know that the LORD is God.
It is he who made us, and we are his;
we are his people, the sheep of his pasture.

PSALM 100:3 NIV

Slow down. Let's go through this together, line by line. *Know that the Lord is God.* "I do," we say. But do we live like it? He *is God.* Sovereign, perfect, Lord of All. What would our day look like if we kept this at the front of our awareness? How light would our burdens become if we knew it was he who carries them?

It is he who made us, and we are his. Again, we say we know this, but again, do we live like it is true? We are *his.* How often, how very often, we behave as though we belong only to ourselves! We hear him say "This way, my love," as we continue to race down our own path. All the while, we wonder why life is so hard. How much easier would the journey be if we turned around and followed him?

Father, I acknowledge you today as Lord. I lay down the struggle and surrender my burdens to you. I turn from the path of my own choosing and run joyfully into your pasture. I am wholly yours. Thank you for lighting my path. Thank you for welcoming me home.

LAID LOW

My soul clings to the dust;
Revive me according to your word.
> PSALM 119:25 NKJV

How does this Scripture sit with you? Your reaction says much about the condition of your spirit. If you felt sympathy and compassion for the psalmist, even if times are tough, you are still strong enough to recognize greater despair than your own. Things are better for you than perhaps you realize.

If these words pierced your soul and felt like a cry from your own heart, you, dear one, are laid low. As your soul clings to the dust, take care not to let the ground claim you. Reach up for the hand of God. Hang on to the many wonderful promises in his Word. He will revive you. He will sustain you. He has beautiful plans for you, even now. Believe it, and feel your spirit rise.

Dear Lord, from the dust, laid low and clinging to none but the tiniest specks of hope, I call on you and you respond. You lift me up, and heal my body. You speak your truth, and revive my soul. Thank you, Father, for your life-giving Word.

YOUR WAYS

Keep me from looking at worthless things.
Let me live by your word.
PSALM 119:37 NCV

Think of a food you enjoyed as a child that you no longer find
palatable, or a childhood game so simple you can scarcely believe
how many hours you once whiled away, enthralled. Where before
we couldn't even taste extra sugar, our faces now contort from the
unnecessary sweetness. Tic-Tac-Toe is only fun if you go first, and
even then only for a round or two. With maturity comes discernment.

Examine your current life through God's eyes. Are there things
clamoring for your attention that, when held up to the lens of
eternity with the Father, lose their luster? Might some of the
discontentment we feel in our daily lives be eliminated simply by
losing our taste for things that don't matter anyway?

Lord, I pray these words over my life: turn my eyes from
looking at worthless things! I want to follow your gaze and see
what you see. I know yours is the way of life, and it's life—real
life—that I crave.

IN A SEASON OF SUFFERING

My comfort in my suffering is this:
Your promise preserves my life.
PSALM 119:50 NIV

It isn't easy in the valley. In a season of suffering, our feet are heavy, the path rocky and rough. To place one foot in front of the other, to take another step forward, requires all our focus. It leaves little room for anything else. Cling to these five words as you go.

Left. *Your promise preserves my life.* Right. *Your promise preserves my life.* Left. *Your promise preserves my life...*

Lord, I'm in the valley. It's deep, dark, and low. My feet feel leaden, my soul dry. I can't see you, yet I know you are there. I suffer, but your promise is my comfort. It sustains my life. And today, that is enough.

THE GIFT IN THE STRUGGLE

My suffering was good for me,
for it taught me to pay attention to your decrees.
  PSALM 119:71 NLT

In the midst of a struggle, passages like this may seem unbelievable, their sentiments unattainable. *How could I ever see this situation as good? That's great for the psalmist, but I don't see myself ever being glad for this affliction.*

Another way to take in these words is as encouragement. King David suffered. While writing these psalms, he experienced mortal peril, extreme discipline for his wrong choices, and the complete humbling of his heart. If he could pen these words, perhaps our situation, though currently so heavy, will one day reveal itself as a blessing too.

Lord God, I won't pretend to enjoy my suffering. You'd see right through my empty words, anyway. I'm not strong enough to thank you for painful lessons while in the midst of them, but I do know that you love me, and that you intend only good for me. I cling to this truth and look forward to the day I see the gift in this struggle.

THE PATH TO PEACE

Great peace have those who love Your law,
And nothing causes them to stumble.
  PSALM 119:165 NKJV

If there were a simple formula for perfect peace, would you follow it? According to this Scripture, there is. Peace belongs to those who love the law of the Lord. How can that be? Isn't rule-following nit-picky and exhausting?

Yes, rule-following is exhausting, but mercifully, it is not the same thing as loving the law. To love God's law is to trust his will for our lives, and to desire to please him above all else. When this is the focus of our hearts, we needn't keep a list or check up on ourselves. He will keep our hearts in line with his—therefore, we can be certain our steps are sure.

Lord, as I desire more and more to walk in step with you, I am learning to trust your will. Help me to see your law as a path to peace, and keep me from stumbling as I go.

GET WISE

The beginning of wisdom is this: Get wisdom,
and whatever else you get, get insight.

PROVERBS 4:7 NRSV

Sign here. Circle your answer. Stop. In a world that can be hard to
navigate, isn't it great when instructions are clear? The Word of God
contains its fair share of poetry and symbolism, but sometimes the
message requires no interpretation whatsoever. These are the things
the Father wants to be sure we *all* understand. As a million things
clamor for our attention, the ones that matter most are the ones he
makes the clearest.

Look at the passage above. If you want to be wise, the first thing
to understand is this. you *want* to be wise! Getting wisdom is a big
deal; in fact, it's the key to everything. As you move through your
day today, whatever tough choices you face, take comfort in knowing
that when it really matters, you'll know.

Father God, open my eyes to opportunities to grow in wisdom
today; the world is confusing, but your way is clear. Thank
you for making the things I most need to know so easy to
understand.

ROCK SOLID

The rain came down, the streams rose, and the winds blew and beat against that house; yet it did not fall, because it had its foundation on the rock.

MATTHEW 7:25 NIV

A storm has become a consistent metaphor for a difficult situation, and considering the passage above, it's easy to see why. Issues pour down upon us, calamities rise up around us, and problems beat up against us—sometimes all at once. Such times are often when we learn how solid our own foundation is. If we are relying on our own strength, or even other people, for our stability, we may find ourselves flattened when the clouds recede.

A life structured on faith in God, built upon his Word, and assembled with his truth is solid, able to withstand even the strongest of storms. We may find ourselves rattled, with a few shattered windows or even a hole in the roof, but we are standing. With Christ as our foundation, strong and certain, we remain upright.

Lord Jesus, I build my house upon you. Your Word, your sacrifice, and your grace are the pillars of my life. Because this is true, I know that no matter what I face, I will not fall. I claim and believe this truth today, Jesus, in your name.

THE ME YOU SEE

Mary responded, "I am the Lord's servant. May everything you have said about me come true." And then the angel left her.

LUKE 1:38 NLT

At first reading, or even after many readings of the above passage, we are impressed by Mary's obedience. Faced with the extraordinary command to bear God's Son—as an unwed teenager—she agrees without hesitation. Upon closer inspection, however, something else stands out: her hope. "May everything you have said about me come true."

The Lord sees us, each and all. He knows every good thing about you, all your potential is laid out before him like a beautiful promise. He speaks about you like a proud papa, extolling your gifts. Claim Mary's line for yourself today; make it your prayer.

Father God, may everything you have said about me come true. Empower and embolden me to explore every desire you have placed in my heart, to develop and use every talent for your glory. Help me to believe in the me you see, and help me to see her, too.

SO MUCH LOVE

As the murderous stones came hurtling at him, Stephen prayed, "Lord Jesus, receive my spirit." And he fell to his knees, shouting, "Lord, don't charge them with this sin!" and with that, he died.

ACTS 7:59-60 TLB

At the hands of a murderous mob, do you think your last words would be a prayer for those throwing the stones? Even with his final breath, Stephen modeled the kind of life Jesus wants for his followers. But what an overwhelming charge: pray for our enemies? Really?

We are not admonished to pray for our persecutors for their own sakes, but for ours. Filled with the Holy Spirit, Stephen's heart contained an otherwise impossible degree of love, and an unfathomable degree of peace. Not even the pain of hurtling stones could contain his spirit. Through his manner of dying, Stephen showed his murderers—and us—a beautiful way to live.

Lord, fill me with the peace of Stephen, allow me to be so wrapped in your love, that no matter what life throws at me, I can only feel you. Place so much love in my heart that I simply cannot contain it, so much that it extends even to those who would harm me.

THE BEST IS YET TO COME

"Eye has not seen, nor ear heard,
Nor have entered into the heart of man
The things which God has prepared for those who love Him."
  1 CORINTHIANS 2:9 NKJV

Consider the most beautiful thing you've ever seen. Remember, or listen to, the most wonderful song you've ever heard. Imagine the most perfect day possible. Amazing, right?

How much more amazing is it to know that those thoughts and memories are nothing—*nothing*—compared to what God has in store for us? No sight, no sound, no daydream even comes close. And the best part? It's already prepared. A glorious feast for every sense is ready and waiting for us. That's how much we are loved, and that's what we have to look forward to.

Lord, on the days I need a little extra hope, bring this verse to mind. Remind me of how much you adore me, and of all the incredible blessings you want to lavish on me. On the days I need a lot of hope...rain it down.

YOU ARE GIFTED

If the whole body were an eye, where would the hearing be? If the whole body were hearing, where would the sense of smell be? But as it is, God arranged the members in the body, each one of them, as he chose.

1 CORINTHIANS 12:17-18 NRSV

Has a captivating singer, speaker or dancer ever brought up a longing in you to perform at that level, or a brilliant work of art stirred up a desire to create beauty with your own hands? Such temporary feelings are natural; beauty is inspiring! But if we hold onto a desire to possess someone else's gifts, we run the risk of forgetting about— or never discovering—our own.

Spend some time thinking about what makes you special. If this makes you uncomfortable, or if you aren't sure, recall a time you felt particularly alive, when things just seemed to be clicking. What were you doing? Begin there, and ask God to show you how to do it for his glory.

Father, everything from your hands is good and special, and that includes me. Help me to remember this, especially on the days it feels like everyone has more to offer than I do. Light a fire in me to explore, develop, and use my uniqueness to glorify you.

A GREATER WORK

I begged the Lord three times to take this problem away from me. But he said to me, "My grace is enough for you. When you are weak, my power is made perfect in you."

2 CORINTHIANS 12:8-9 NCV

Your child makes the team, then breaks a bone and spends the season on the bench. Your parent contracts an illness, and despite your prayers, God's not taking it away. You sign up to run a marathon for your favorite charity, then tear your hamstring on a training run. What is going on? Does God want us to suffer?

God never wishes harm on anyone, but he does use our afflictions to demonstrate his power and multiply our effectiveness. Had you not torn your hamstring, you'd be just another runner on marathon Sunday. But on crutches, hobbling through a 2K run, you attract the attention of the media and thanks to a video interview that goes viral, you're able to share your cause with millions. The next time you find yourself weakened and vulnerable, look for how God might be using your circumstances to do a greater work.

Lord God, help me to see my difficulties with the clarity and faith of Paul! Your grace is enough, and if weakness is what you require of me right now, let me boast in it and bring you glory.

FEBRUARY

According to your steadfast love remember me,
for the sake of your goodness, O Lord!

PSALM 25:7 ESV

SWEEP MY HEART

"Don't sin by letting anger control you." Don't let the sun go down while you are still angry, for anger gives a foothold to the devil.

EPHESIANS 4:26-27 NLT

Sometimes, even reading a verse like this can cause the hairs on the backs of our necks to rise. "That's easy for him to say; but if he knew what she did to me…" And besides, how are we supposed to prevent our emotions? Great news: we're not. It's not sin to feel anger; no emotion is sinful. It's how we handle them that can entrap us in a spiral of destructive actions and guilt.

Getting angry is one thing, but choosing to stay that way—plotting revenge, gossiping, and living with the shame of our choices—is something else. We would never knowingly invite the devil into our lives, but when we hang onto negativity, that's exactly what we're doing. Use Paul's warning as an encouragement to release anyone you might be harboring anger against, and enjoy the resulting lightness in your heart.

Father, sweep my heart! I want to be controlled by your Spirit, not by my emotions. Help me let go of any obvious anger and reveal any hidden resentment, so I can be free to experience all the joy of a life lived in your presence.

GIVE HIM YOUR WORRY

Do not be anxious about anything, but in every situation, by prayer and petition, with thanksgiving, present your requests to God. And the peace of God, which transcends all understanding, will guard your hearts and your minds in Christ Jesus.

PHILIPPIANS 4:6-7 NIV

Because this passage is one of the more familiar in Scripture, it's possible to miss the huge promise imbedded in the second half. God's unimaginable peace will protect your heart and mind. Whoa.

All we have to do—the one thing—is give our worries to God. In exchange, he will grant us the peace of Jesus himself; a peace, we are told, we can't even wrap our minds around. Can it really be so simple? Absolutely. But does that mean it's easy? Worry is sticky, and we can become so familiar with it, it starts to feel like a friend. Like gum in our hair, or sap on our hands, some extra effort is required to get rid of it. But oh, read that second verse again. How very worth the effort the payoff—the peace of Christ—will be!

Lord Jesus, so often I come to you for help, but I do not leave my concerns at your feet. Thank you for the reminder of what I can trade those worries for—your peace! Guard my heart and mind, Jesus, and free me from all anxiety.

CLAIM YOUR PEACE

I know how to live when I am poor, and I know how to live when I have plenty. I have learned the secret of being happy at any time in everything that happens, when I have enough to eat and when I go hungry, when I have more than I need and when I do not have enough. I can do all things through Christ, because he gives me strength.

PHILIPPIANS 4:12-13 NCV

Can you imagine experiencing the same level of happiness and contentment upon learning your job is being eliminated as you would upon getting an unexpected raise or promotion? The implication of these verses is simply extraordinary.

The wonderful news is that we can all experience it. The contentedness that comes from knowing Christ is in unlimited supply; there's more than enough to go around. In fact, the more of us who claim it, the more his strength, peace, and happiness increase. Whether it's a day of plenty or a day of want, claim your peace and share the hope it gives you.

Jesus, I've learned the secret to happiness and I want in! I invite you to take over my emotions, sending contentment into every part of my life so that no matter what circumstances I face, I face them with your strength and I experience nothing but your joy.

SIGHT UNSEEN

Though you have not seen him, you love him; and even though you do not see him now, you believe in him and are filled with an inexpressible and glorious joy.

1 PETER 1:8 NIV

How did you first fall in love with Jesus? Unlike human love, one of the great mysteries of faith is how we can know so surely and love so deeply he whom we've never actually seen. But we can. We do.

One of the great rewards of faith is the "inexpressible and glorious joy" the Holy Spirit places in our hearts the moment we believe. Have you claimed your joy today?

Father, as I meditate today on all the ways I know you are real, allow your Spirit to fill me once again with the inexpressible, glorious joy that comes only from loving you.

SEEK TO DO GOOD

See that none of you repays evil for evil, but always seek to do good to one another and to all.

1 THESSALONIANS 5:15 NRSV

For a small child, a shove from another gets a shove in return. A cruel word, a cruel word. They can't help it; self-defense is an inborn reaction to an attack. What these little ones don't know yet, but learn quickly, is that regardless of who strikes first, both are punished. In our weaker moments, this natural impulse can rear its destructive head in our adult lives as well. "She said what? Oh, really? Well let me tell you about her marriage..."

Here's the problem. When we allow ugliness into our hearts, we allow it to take up residence, and it invites its friends—bitterness, loneliness, and rage—to move in as well. They spread out, taking up more and more space, crowding out the peace, patience, and goodness of Jesus. This is why we must "seek to do good to one another and to all," not because we'll be punished, but so our hearts will be filled with the life-giving gifts of the Spirit.

Holy Spirit, fill me with your fruit! With the love, joy, peace, patience, kindness, goodness, faithfulness, gentleness, and self-control you bring, no matter what is done to me, I can respond as I should. You are all I want in my heart; rid me of everything else.

Yes, Please!

With this in mind, we constantly pray for you, that our God may make you worthy of his calling, and that by his power he may bring to fruition your every desire for goodness and your every deed prompted by faith.

2 THESSALONIANS 1:11 NIV

There is so much to be encouraged by in this wonderful prayer from Paul to the Thessalonians! Do you have a group of women to pray and study the Word with? If you don't, pray that the Father would lead you to them, then keep your eyes and heart open. If you do, you know how beautiful it is to be always in the prayers of someone, and to have someone always in yours. Praying for others takes our focus off ourselves and blesses us in unique and surprising ways.

Even more encouraging is the content of Paul's prayer: that we be "worthy of his calling," and that all we "desire for goodness" and everything we do "prompted by faith" would succeed. Yes, please!

Oh Lord, yes, please! I want to be worthy of your calling, to be equipped to do all I can to bring you glory. I pray that all I do to express, share, and increase my love for you would succeed. For all who are reading this, I pray the same. Make us a force of light and goodness in this world. Bless our actions and increase our faith.

MORE THAN GOLD

These troubles come to prove that your faith is pure. This purity of faith is worth more than gold, which can be proved to be pure by fire but will ruin. But the purity of your faith will bring you praise and glory and honor when Jesus Christ is shown to you.

1 PETER 1:7 NCV

We can waste much of our lives trying to answer the "whys" of our most difficult times. Most of the answers we seek will not be revealed to us until we meet the Lord in heaven, but Scriptures such as this one from Peter provide lovely encouragement while we wait. We know gold is precious—so precious it's a universal standard for measuring the entire world's wealth. Here, we are told that faith that withstands troubled times is worth more than all the gold on earth.

Holding strong to God's promises regardless of what struggles we face affords us an invaluable reward: the praise, honor, and glory of Jesus himself. This doesn't mean our difficulty is a test *assigned by* God, but the outcome—a faith that withstands the fire—is *used by* him to bless us beyond imagining.

Lord, I invite you to use my pain, present and future, as a proving ground for my faith. Allow my troubles to strengthen my trust in you; allow difficulty to increase my reliance on you. When you prove yourself faithful, as you always do, may I grow to love you more and more.

THE WHOLE HOT MESS

Cast all your anxiety on him, because he cares for you.
1 PETER 5:7 NRSV

Pressures, frustrations, and injustices have a way of building up.
Thankfully, we usually recognize it happening before we lose it in
the checkout lane. We call a friend and open the steam valve on our
emotions. "I just need to vent," we say. It does feel good to release
the pressure, but the situations that led to the buildup are still ours
to carry.

The Lord is always available, and like a dear friend, we can vent to
him any time. But if a sounding board is all we allow God to be, we
are missing out on one of his greatest blessings. He wants us to shed
our burdens completely. As much as your loved ones care, they don't
want your pile of bills, surly teenager, or demanding boss. Only Jesus
cares that deeply. Only Jesus invites you to give him the whole, hot
mess. So why don't we?

My Lord, my confidante, you know my struggles, and you know
when it all becomes too much. You adore me; you long to ease
my burden. I don't know why I insist on carrying the whole
load by myself, refusing your help. Help me grasp the depth of
your love and to gratefully let you take over.

IN HIS LIGHT

In him was life, and that life was the light of all mankind.
The light shines in the darkness, and the darkness has not
overcome it.

JOHN 1:4-5 NIV

Unless you're trying to sleep, what's the first thing you look for in the
dark? Light. A switch, a source, some way to get through the darkness.
Figuratively speaking, the principle is the same. Walking through
emotional darkness of any kind, we need only look for the light.
Today's verse, so eloquently expressed by the Apostle John, reminds us
of the ultimate source—Jesus, the light of all mankind.

No darkness, whether fear, or pain, or sin, or loss, can conquer the
light of his Word. His love never fails, his promises are forever, and his
grace is ours. Whatever we face, whatever we've done, nothing can
claim us or take us from his light.

Lord Jesus, you are light itself. Beautiful and shining, you
cast truth onto lies, hope onto despair, and grace onto sin—
obliterating darkness. You cannot be overcome, and in you,
neither can I.

WORTH IT

Jesus answered, "It was not that this man sinned, or his parents, but that the works of God might be displayed in him."
JOHN 9:3 ESV

Back in Jesus' time, people with afflictions were often thought to be receiving punishment for sin. Upon encountering a man blind from birth, Jesus' disciples made such an assumption and asked Jesus whose sins the man was being punished for. Before restoring the man's sight, Jesus explained punishment had nothing to do with it. He was blind so people—then and for all time—could catch a glimpse of the awesome power of God.

Pain and suffering are no fun, and can feel a whole lot like punishment. In the midst of it, it's tempting to think, "Why can't he display his power on someone else?" But consider this: if you could ask the man Jesus healed if his years of blindness were worth being touched and healed by the Son of God himself, if Jesus' face being the first thing his eyes ever beheld was worth years of preceding darkness, what do you think he would say?

Lord, I know my troubles aren't punishment. You took care of my sin once and for all on the cross. Help me remain open to your works. If I need to suffer for a time, let me suffer gladly, knowing the touch of your hands—and the sight of your face—are worth any earthly trouble I face.

HEART DIRECTIONS

May the Lord direct your hearts into the love of God and into the patience of Christ.

2 THESSALONIANS 3:5 NKJV

Children have an amusing (and occasionally terrifying) habit of running ahead of their parents, only to realize they don't actually know where they are going. Eventually it dawns on them, and they stop. They wait. To find a place you've never been, you need directions.

This blessing from 2 Thessalonians is a lovely reminder of this principle as it applies to our hearts. How often do you run ahead of God, pursuing relationships, accomplishments, answers? Lurching forward, not glancing to either side, anxious to be there already, you look up to find yourself in unfamiliar territory. Let it dawn on you. *I don't know where I'm going.* Stop, and wait. Allow the Lord to speak direction into your heart, filling it with his love. Let him grace you with Christ's patience, infusing the journey with meaning.

Lord, my heart needs directions. I think I know where I'm going and what I need, but so often I end up lost, confused, and uncertain. Fill me with your love, God. Pour your patience into me, Jesus. Direct my heart and lead me to you.

HE WILL BE FOUND

"I will be found by you," says the LORD. "I will end your captivity and restore your fortunes. I will gather you out of the nations where I sent you and will bring you home again to your own land."

JEREMIAH 29:14 NLT

Lost. It's an uncomfortable word. Being lost is unnerving, and losing something is unsettling. Losing someone: unbearable. Losing God? Unthinkable. Though they were sent far away from him for many years, Jeremiah 29 contains God's beautiful words of comfort to his beloved Israel. "I will be found by you...I will bring you home again."

Many believers encounter a season where God might feel far away, or even lost. The relief of finding what we've misplaced is nothing— nothing—compared to the incomprehensible joy of reuniting with the Lord. He will be found! He intends good for you. He adores you, and if you continue to seek his face and claim his promises for your life, he will bring you home again.

Father, there are days I fear I've lost you. I know it isn't true, but I can't feel your presence or find your peace. I never want to be away from you, Lord. Find me, Father. Draw me near. Bring me home.

FREE TO REST

The fear of the LORD leads to life;
then one rests content, untouched by trouble.

PROVERBS 19:23 NIV

Contentment and freedom from trouble sound great, but what does it mean to fear the Lord? Aren't we covered by Jesus' sacrifice, forgiven for our sins, adopted into the family, and welcomed into heaven? What's there to fear? Consider the ocean: vast and deep, beautiful and bountiful, yet undeniably dangerous. Foolish enough to jump alone into the middle, one would never expect to survive. Fear in this context means not to expect harm, but to respect power.

Respecting the depth and force of the ocean, we have the wisdom to remain on the ship. We rest content on the deck, untouched by the creatures of the deep. Respecting the full sovereignty of God, we are less prone to the troubles that arise from surrender to temptation, leaving us free to rest in his embrace.

Lord, I am in awe of you. When I think of your power, of all you've done and will do, I can only stand back in amazement. Allow my mind to stay here, meditating on your greatness. Keep me here in your arms—safe, alive, and filled with peace.

SPEAKING TRUTH

An open rebuke
is better than hidden love!
Wounds from a sincere friend
are better than many kisses from an enemy.
PROVERBS 27:5-6 NLT

You're angry, hurt, disappointed, and confused. *How could she say that? How could he do it?* She doesn't even know you heard. He has no idea you know. You know you should talk about it—confront them, but confrontation makes you uncomfortable. Just imagining the conversation makes you queasy. So you pull away.

Perhaps the only thing harder than hearing something we don't want to hear is telling it to someone we love. But if we don't tell them, if we don't give them an opportunity to apologize and make things right, can we really claim to love them? Confrontation means you care. The truth, even when it's ugly, will come from someone who genuinely loves you.

Lord, help me to recognize any hurts I'm holding onto, and give me the courage to speak the truth and heal my hurting relationships. Draw me to people who love me enough to tell me the truth, even when it's hard to hear.

Keep Going

Whether you turn to the right or to the left, your ears will hear
a voice behind you, saying, "This is the way; walk in it."
ISAIAH 30:21 NIV

*Should I change jobs? Is this the one? Is now the right time to have
a baby? What should I do?* Sound familiar? Decisions, especially
the really big ones, are so much easier when we feel certain. If only
there could be a big sign and arrow blinking over the right choice:
"Pick me!" God gave us free will; we have the right to make our own
choices, so we can pretty much count on not seeing any neon.

This doesn't mean he's not guiding us, however. A closer reading of
the Scripture offers an important detail when seeking God's direction.
The voice—his voice—will be *behind* us. Think of learning to ride a
bicycle. Where do you want your teacher? Standing at the end of
the block waving his arms and yelling, "Here! Over here!" or running
alongside you, speaking encouragement and reassurance right into
your ear? "Yes, that's it! You're doing it! Now keep going. Keep going."

Thank you, Father; I see it now. Instead of sitting, waiting for
you to tell me where to go, I just need to go—somewhere,
anywhere—and listen for your voice. You're here, keeping me
steady, guiding my way. Help me hear you, Lord, then fill me
with the courage to go where you send me.

THE ETERNAL YOU

When you pass through the waters, I will be with you;
and through the rivers, they shall not overwhelm you;
when you walk through fire you shall not be burned,
and the flame shall not consume you.

ISAIAH 43:2 NRSV

This life will try you. You might be in the river right now: chest deep, soaked through, barely steady against the current. This world will hurt you. Perhaps you can smell smoke this very day, feel the heat at your back and under your feet. Things happen—hard things—and no one is immune.

Not immune, but as his child, you are protected. He's in the river too, guiding you to the bank. He's right here in the inferno, fireproof and covering you. These lines are not an exemption from feeling pain or being broken; our Father is protecting the eternal you. Your heart can not be overwhelmed. Your soul can not be consumed. You are his. You are forever.

Lord, I fear because I forget this life isn't the whole story. I struggle because I forget who keeps me afloat. Even if the river takes my breath, it won't take me. Even if the fire gets to my flesh—and I admit this scares me—it won't get to me. I am eternal, because I am yours.

CONSIDER HIS HAND

Behold, I am doing a new thing;
now it springs forth, do you not perceive it?
I will make a way in the wilderness
and rivers in the desert.
ISAIAH 43:19 ESV

Hiking through a state or national park on a well-worn, carefully laid out trail, one doesn't consider all the work that went into creating that path. Wander off the path for just a minute or two, and you start to gain an appreciation for the vast amount of effort, the countless hours required to remove the branches, brambles, and roots along the way. Flipping on a faucet, we don't often give much thought to the source of the water, or the many places in the world where a single faucet would be nothing short of a miracle to an entire community.

God's work in our lives, though just as intricate, can go similarly unnoticed. Take some time this morning to consider every obstacle he's removed for you to have the life you have. Marvel at how he can pull a spring up out of nothing, sustaining you just because he wants to. Just because he loves you. He's amazing.

Lord, you are incredible. When I stop to consider just my own life, the millions of obstacles you've removed and the continual sustenance you've provided, it blows my mind. How deeply I am loved, how carefully you consider me! Thank you, God, for all you have done and will do.

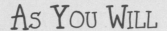

As You Will

I rise before dawn and cry for help;
I hope in your words.
PSALM 119:147 ESV

For an early-morning person, these words are relatable, and perhaps even unremarkable. For those who favor the snooze button, rising before dawn sounds highly overrated. So how do those who love their sleep get past the opening phrase and lay claim to the power and promise in this verse?

They meet the day. They open their eyes, and their thoughts go straight to the Lord. Before anyone or anything has an opportunity to crowd their thoughts with obligation, worry, or entertainment, they bring themselves authentic and unadulterated before God. They go to his Word, and let him speak to them there. They find their hope there before anything else finds them.

Help me, Father God. I run to meet you. Help me love, listen, and learn well today. Before anything or anyone else can say a word, let me hear from you. This is where my hope lies, in these first minutes, when we are all there is. See me as I am, and make me as you will.

GO TO THE GARDEN

Then he said to them, "My soul is overwhelmed with sorrow to the point of death. Stay here and keep watch with me."
MATTHEW 26:38 NIV

This passage, written about the night Jesus was taken into custody, reveals a few very tender, very human things about our Lord. First, Jesus was sad. In fact, he was "overwhelmed with sorrow." Take that in. He gets it! Jesus, the Son of God, knows exactly what it feels like to be in the depths of despair. He won't be disappointed in you for failing to see the bright side. He's been there.

Also, in his moment of greatest sorrow, Jesus needed people. He brought his three closest friends to the garden with him that night. We were not meant to do this alone. Not any of it. If the Lord himself needed those he loved the most when feeling his worst, so do we. Trust your people with your pain. And when they trust you with theirs, treasure that trust as a gift from God.

Lord God, thank you for your Son. He died for me, and now he shows me how to live. He reminds me that it's okay to bring you my sadness, and he reminds me I need my people. Who would go to the garden with me, hit their knees beside me? Help me see them, and make me the kind of friend who will fall to my knees with them.

A Guarded Heart

Above all else, guard your heart,
for everything you do flows from it.
PROVERBS 4:23 NIV

The heart is a funny thing. It tends to get tripped up easily, and tricked into wandering away from what the Lord wants for it. We start out seeking him in all we do, and then bit by bit we are lured away from the straight and narrow, until we can't even see the path for the forest any more. It's never a huge leap off that path; rather, a slow process that leads us further from his desires for us until we are so entangled in our mess that our hearts begin to break with the weight of it.

There's a reason why the Bible tells us to protect our hearts! God knows how susceptible we are to attack. We need to pray for safekeeping over this most precious piece of us.

Lord, help me guard my heart. Show me the ways in which I am vulnerable to attack and the stumbling blocks to which I am prone. Give me shelter in your Word and truth. Thank you for being my shield and my armor against what the enemy wants for me.

HESITANT

All that the Father gives me will come to me, and whoever comes to me I will never cast out.

JOHN 6:37 ESV

Even though God's arms are always open to us, sometimes we are hesitant to go to him. Despite his promises of acceptance and love, we feel embarrassed by our sin. We feel unworthy to sit in his presence. We feel inadequate. Certainly he will turn us away. Our shame causes us to hide from the one who loves us the most.

But God says that we are always welcome. There is no sin great enough for him to reject us. He loves us in spite of our many mistakes, grievances, and inadequacies. When we are at the end of ourselves, when we can't even bear to look at ourselves, that is where we find Jesus. It's in our hour of complete brokenness that he is there. He picks up the shattered pieces and calls us beautiful.

Thank you, Jesus, that when I say I am unlovable, you challenge that lie and draw yourself closer to me. My sin and brokenness does not deter you. I am thankful that you accept me for all that I am, and all that I am not.

A Humble Heart

"Let the one who boasts, boast in the Lord." For it is not the one who commends himself who is approved, but the one whom the Lord commends.

2 CORINTHIANS 10:17-18 ESV

Not much feels better than receiving a sincere compliment. Isn't it great when your hard work is noticed, or your new hair cut is a hit, or your recipe was loved at the party? When you don't get the credit you feel you deserved, it can be tempting to say something. You want to let others know about the fantastic qualities you think they may have missed in you.

But the Bible cautions us against giving in to the temptation to brag. Instead, let's tell others about all the amazing qualities to be found in a relationship with the Lord! Every talent we've been given, and everything we've achieved, has been because he has given us these gifts. Let's boast about how awesome he truly is!

Lord, you really are incredible, and you've given me so much. You've given me gifts and talents, and I've been able to accomplish more because of you than I ever would have on my own. I pray for a humble heart in all that I do.

GROUNDED

"I am leaving you with a gift—peace of mind and heart. And the peace I give is a gift the world cannot give. So don't be troubled or afraid."

JOHN 14:27 NLT

When stress hits us, the most logical thing to do is fix or remove whatever factor in our life is causing the stress. Rather than leaning into God, often our reaction is to become anxious, fearful, and agitated. In that state of mind it is easy to make decisions that are not well thought through. Instead of relieving the stress, we only feed it, making the situation even worse.

By releasing the desire to manipulate the situation, and acknowledging that God is in control, peace floods our hearts and calms our spirits. Knowing that the God we serve is good, loving, and all-powerful is the key to feeling grounded in rocky situations. Being able to trust him with our stress is a gift.

Father, thank you that you are God and I am not. I am grateful that you are able to calm my spirits so easily. Help me be willing to release my need to control into your hands.

STEADFAST WISDOM

This is my prayer: that your love may abound more and more in knowledge and depth of insight, so that you may be able to discern what is best and may be pure and blameless for the day of Christ.

PHILIPPIANS 1:9-10 NIV

One of the most beautiful things about the Bible is that we are able to use the words written there, words given to the writers directly from the Lord himself, to pray over our lives. It's such a powerful thing to be able to use the same prayer that thousands have prayed for thousands of years and know that it still applies to our lives today.

Who among us couldn't use some more knowledge, insight, and discernment? These things aren't fads that are going away any time soon. Let's continue to take the words given to us all those years ago, and apply them to the modern day.

Lord, I want to be pure and blameless, and ready for the day Christ is coming back. Thank you for the gift of wisdom. I pray that you would give me insight into your will for me each and every day. I praise you for the gift of your Word!

JOIN TOGETHER

May God, who gives this patience and encouragement, help you live in complete harmony with each other, as is fitting for followers of Christ Jesus. Then all of you can join together with one voice, giving praise and glory to God, the Father of our Lord Jesus Christ.

ROMANS 15:5-6 NLT

Often it can feel like we are in competition with those in our lives. Even among fellow believers there can be an undertone of judgment and disapproval. But that isn't what God had in mind for us. He built us to be in relationship with one another with one goal in mind: to live our lives in worship together.

Isn't it a lovely reminder to know that God gives us endurance and encouragement? That through him we can be of one mind with our fellow Christians? Together, we can use our voice to glorify him as was intended.

Lord, thank you for the reminder that you want us to lift one another up and work together rather than pull each other down. Help me to be someone who encourages those around me.

NEVER ALONE

Who shall separate us from the love of Christ? Shall
tribulation, or distress, or persecution, or famine, or nakedness,
or danger, or sword?

ROMANS 8:35 ESV

There's an underlying theme laced throughout the words of the Bible.
It's a truth you can stand on whenever life threatens to pull you
down. When the enemy whispers in your ear, and all you can hear is
the lie that you are unloved, alone, and too weak to get through your
day, tell yourself with certainty that it's just not true. The Bible tells
us that we are never alone. In fact, it says quite simply that nothing
can separate us from the love of Christ.

Trouble and hardship will come our way. But through it all, the love of
our Lord and Savior is there to rely upon. We can conquer more than
we realize because he is there to fight our battles with us.

Lord, thank you for loving me through the worst life has for
me.

LOVELY AND PURE

Finally, brothers and sisters, whatever is true, whatever is noble, whatever is right, whatever is pure, whatever is lovely, whatever is admirable—if anything is excellent or praiseworthy—think about such things.

PHILIPPIANS 4:8 NIV

It's easy to let our minds begin to race the moment we get out of bed. We are designed to be doers and to check off the many things on our list. We can be swept up in the stress of the to-dos and forget to start our days with the peace and tranquility that comes from spending time with the Lord.

But oh, just look at the beauty of the words in Philippians! How amazing to start our day thinking of what's pure, true, noble, admirable, excellent, and praiseworthy. And once our day has begun on that note, how much easier it is to continue on in the same vein. We may be doers, but we have also been designed to enjoy what's lovely, so let's not forget to spend time thinking about that!

Lord, thank you for the beauty in my life. There is so much that is excellent and praiseworthy! You are the giver of all of these things, and for that I am grateful.

OUR ROCK

There is no one holy like the LORD,
Indeed, there is no one besides You,
Nor is there any rock like our God.

1 SAMUEL 2:2 NASB

Most of us have been blessed by special relationships in our lives. We are surrounded by friends and family that love us. These are people we can turn to in times of trouble and pain. And it can be tempting to allow these people to feel like a rock: a stabilizer. As soon as something happens, we run to them and ask for their strength to get us through. But the Bible tells us that there is no rock like our God. He's the best; there's no one else that can take his place.

When we start to worry, or become afraid, or experience difficulty, our first source of comfort should be the Lord. He is so good to us! No matter what it is we are going through, he will be there for us. There is simply no one like him.

Lord, I give you my burdens. I'm so thankful that you are my rock and my daily source of strength. I pray that I would remember to turn to you first in all that I do.

MARCH

How kind the LORD is!

How good he is!

So merciful, this God of ours!

PSALM 116:5 NLT

MIGHTY GOD

Ah, Lord GOD! Behold, You have made the heavens and the earth by Your great power and outstretched arm. There is nothing too hard for You.

JEREMIAH 32:17 NKJV

There are days in which you may feel that the load you are carrying is simply too heavy. There is a lot on your plate, and there is no way you will be able to clear it. On days like that, take heart from the words in Jeremiah: the Lord made the heavens and the earth. That was no small feat. If he can accomplish such great and mighty things, think of what he can do in your life. He will carry you through!

Nothing is too hard for God. *Nothing.* It doesn't say that things aren't too hard with the exception of whatever you have going on and the struggles you are going through! No! There is *nothing* he can't handle. He loves you. You were built for relationship with him, and that relationship means that he will lift you up and be there for you when everything seems to be falling apart. Trust in that knowledge today.

Lord, I know that nothing is too hard for you. Thank you for carrying my burdens for me.

No Greater Love

We know what real love is from Christ's example in dying for us. And so we also ought to lay down our lives for our Christian brothers.

1 JOHN 3:16 TLB

There is no greater example of love than that of Christ Jesus. He gave it all for love—leaving the beauty of heaven so that we could spend eternity with him. We are called to emulate Christ's love. So why is it so difficult for us to lay down our own lives for others? Why do we hold so tightly to our comforts and our treasures when we know we should be making a sacrifice?

Let's look for the ways in our lives that we can lay it all down for our fellow brothers and sisters. While we may not all be called to die for the kingdom, we are all called to a life of sacrifice. Let's discover what this means for ourselves and be open to seeing opportunities to give it all.

Father, I pray I would be willing to give up everything I have for you and look for ways to do so. Thank you for the ultimate gift you've given me in laying down your life.

COURAGEOUS

"Have I not commanded you? Be strong and courageous. Do not be afraid; do not be discouraged, for the Lord your God will be with you wherever you go."

JOSHUA 1:9 NIV

At some point each of us will experience fear. There will be something we go through that will push us to the brink, and we may become afraid that we just will not make it through. But there is truth that we can rely on whenever we come to this point. We are never alone: God will get us through.

We can be strong and we can be courageous. Because the Lord himself will give us the power to do so. He promises never to leave us, and never to abandon us in the midst of our trials and tribulations. No matter what life throws at us, we can persevere because we have the strongest and most courageous one standing behind us.

Lord, thank you for giving me courage when I can't find it on my own. I pray that you will help me overcome my fears, and that I will rest in the knowledge that you will never leave me. Thank you for your strength.

United as One

If there is any encouragement in Christ, any comfort from love, any participation in the Spirit, any affection and sympathy, complete my joy by being of the same mind, having the same love, being in full accord and of one mind.

PHILIPPIANS 2:1-2 ESV

One. It sounds like a pretty lonely number, doesn't it? But it's quite the opposite when we are united with others, and become as one. When we come together with other Christians, we are called to be in unison in our thinking and our spirit. Does it mean that we will align perfectly in our political beliefs or our ideas on other touchy subjects? No! But it does mean that we should be working together to build the kingdom of Christ, and to show his love to others.

We spend so much time fighting about where we differ. Instead, let's find where we are alike! We have one common cause, and that is our Lord and Savior. And in him, we can find community like never before.

Lord, help me to see past my differences with other believers around me and instead find our commonalities so we can be more effective in working together to show your love to the world.

HATE EVIL

You who love the Lord, hate evil!
He protects the lives of his godly people
and rescues them from the power of the wicked.
    PSALM 97:10 NLT

You turn on the news in the morning, or open a newspaper, and every day it's full of the same stories. Atrocities around the world are being committed each day. By now, it's become so much the norm that we are immune to it. Until it affects our lives directly, we often don't even notice it.

But we are asked to hate evil. We aren't told to merely put up with evil, or to make sure that we don't let it bother us. We are supposed to loathe it. What does that mean for us? It means we should be praying for those affected and looking for ways to help. God will deliver them from the hand of the wicked, but he needs his armies here on earth to do their part. Together, let's offer hope to those who are suffering.

Lord, thank you for guarding me from evil. I pray for those who are troubled today, that they may see your light.

EVERLASTING LOVE

The LORD appeared to us in the past, saying:
"I have loved you with an everlasting love;
I have drawn you with unfailing kindness."
JEREMIAH 31:3 NIV

It's easy to believe that we are hard to love. We're full of mistakes, and sometimes just downright crabby. But there is one who loves us regardless of what we've done or said. The Lord tells us plainly that he loves us with an everlasting love. Everlasting literally lasts forever. There is no getting away from his love.

Isn't it amazing that God loves us this way? No matter how we run, or what we do to draw his anger, he will love us right through it? Who else could love like this? Soak in that everlasting love today. Revel in it. You are loved deeply and truly, forevermore.

Father, thank you for loving me regardless of the choices I make. I pray that I would bask in your love today and every day. May your love for me be a reminder to love others well. I lift up those that might be feeling alone and pray they'll come to know your love for them.

Keep Calm

Be not quick in your spirit to become angry,
for anger lodges in the heart of fools.
ECCLESIASTES 7:9 ESV

You get cut off in traffic and it makes you want to scream. The server brings you a lukewarm bowl of soup with a hair in it and your frustration builds. A friend treats you unfairly and your anger bubbles up inside, threatening to spill over in a rage. We've all been in a situation that brings us to the edge, and we just want to snap. If there's one thing that feels worse than anger, it's feeling like a fool. The Bible tells us that's just what we are if we give in to that quick burst of vexation.

It takes nothing less than the power of the Holy Spirit to keep us calm at times. If we want to live a life filled with grace and mercy toward others, he will help us to get there and to respond with kindness when we're feeling mad.

Lord, help me curb my anger! I want to be someone who is a light for your kingdom. I pray others would see you in me as I respond in sticky situations.

DELIGHTFUL

The LORD takes delight in his people;
he crowns the humble with victory.

PSALM 149:4 NIV

If ever there was something to lift your spirits and get you through
the toughest of days, it's the knowledge that the Lord our God takes
delight in you. He tells us so in his Word! He takes pleasure in your
very existence. Our Father created you to be in relationship with him,
and he gets great joy out of it.

Revel in that knowledge today. Embrace the fact that there is one
who loves you and is truly captivated by you. He loves spending time
with you; he wants to go deeper with you each day. Allow him to take
you deeper today! Dive in and experience that delight for yourself.

Father, it makes me smile to know that you delight in your
people. Thank you for loving me like this! I pray I'd remember
the joy that you bring when I'm feeling lost or lonely. I lift up
others who haven't experienced your delight, and pray that
they'd come to know you in a deep and real way. You are truly
glorious, and I'm amazed by you!

DON'T PANIC

So do not fear, for I am with you;
do not be dismayed, for I am your God.
I will strengthen you and help you;
I will uphold you with my righteous right hand.

ISAIAH 41:10 NIV

Are you experiencing something today that is shaking your faith? Do you fear you may not make it through? Take heart! Time and time again, the Lord reassures us that we don't need to be afraid. He tells us he will strengthen us and help us. He's got us in the palm of his hand.

When you start to panic, remember that God has a firm grip on you. He's going to give you the strength you need to get through any situation. Dismay need not be in your vocabulary anymore! He is there to steady you. When you cannot stand on your own, he will be there to uphold you. It's his promise to you!

Lord, thank you for being the steady force in my life. I pray for your strength today! My tendency is toward fear, but I know that I need not be afraid, because you are holding me, keeping me safe and protected from whatever life may throw my way.

ETERNAL GIFT

But the lovingkindness of the LORD is from everlasting to
everlasting on those who fear Him,
And His righteousness to children's children,
To those who keep His covenant
And remember His precepts to do them.
PSALM 103:17-18 NASB

Today, always, and forevermore, the Lord's love will be with you if you
only allow him in. He is sheer mercy and grace. Isn't that amazing?
We don't deserve his love. We fall short daily, and we will never live
up to a life of perfection. Yet he continually doles out more and more
of his abiding love for us. It's always available to us if we choose to
follow his ways and seek a relationship with him.

Turn your face to him today. Let that deep love of his soak in and
wash over you. He knows you inside and out, and he calls you beloved
despite your flaws. Take joy in his love! It's an eternal, precious gift.

Father, I am amazed by your love and how you give it readily.
I do not deserve it, but you still give it freely. I pray I'd never
take that love for granted and that I'd seek to follow you all
the days of my life.

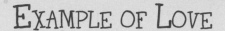

EXAMPLE OF LOVE

A new commandment I give to you, that you love one another;
as I have loved you, that you also love one another. By this all
will know that you are My disciples, if you have love for one
another.

JOHN 13:34-35 NKJV

To be loved is one of the greatest feelings you can have in life.
Knowing someone loves you is like a hug that stays with you all the
time. It's warmth that fills your body and spreads from your center to
your very fingertips. And it's a gift we can pass along to others. The
Lord showed us an extraordinary example of how to love people, and
we can use that illustration of love to give to those around us.

Exemplifying that love is also one of the easiest ways for people to
see Christ in you. Others will look at you and recognize that there
is something different about you, something special, and they'll be
encouraged to find that love for themselves.

Lord, open my eyes to see where I can be an example of your
love today. Let others see you in me in everything I say and do.

HOPE IN HIS WORD

You are my hiding place and my shield;
I hope in your word.

PSALM 119:114 NCV

Hope. It isn't a big word, but there is so much meaning behind those four letters. Hope is a feeling of expectation. It's a desire for a certain outcome. We are designed to live with hope. And thankfully, we can put our hope in someone greater than ourselves—our God. His Word is truth, and all of our expectations and desires can rest in that knowledge.

God is our refuge. He loves us, protects us, and wants the best outcome for us. He gave us his Word, the Bible, as a promise. We can go to it at any time. When hope begins to waver, and doubts creep in, his truth is still there. We have hope for a future because he is our past, present, and forever Lord.

Father, I praise you for being my refuge and shield. Thank you for giving me your Word. I pray that I would turn to you with my every desire and live expectantly, knowing that I can put my hope in you.

NOT A QUITTER

Give thanks to the LORD, for he is good
his love endures forever.
1 CHRONICLES 16:34 NIV

We've all been there before—times get hard, life gets rough, and we just want to say, "I quit!" It's only natural. But there is one who never quits on us. God never gives up on his love for us. For him, it's natural to keep on loving. He loves us with a never-ending, everlasting, beautiful, forever love that sees us through everything.

Isn't that extraordinary? No matter what, God loves us. He doesn't sit on his throne in heaven and say to himself, "Ugh, how annoying! There she is again, off on her own, making poor choices and not listening to me. I'm done with her!" He won't give up on you; you are never alone.

Father, thank you for your enduring love that sees me through thick and thin. I pray I'd remember your love when I feel lost or lonely. I give you all the praise because you are such a good God! I know you will never quit on me.

THE THRILL OF THE HUNT

Whoever pursues righteousness and kindness
will find life and honor.
PROVERBS 21:21 NRSV

Most women love to shop. There's a thrill in hunting down the perfect
item, scoring a great deal, and coming home with fun new treasures.
But there's another kind of hunt that provides an even greater feeling
of excitement. It's the pursuit of a life full of righteousness and love.
A life that's kind and good. When we chase down this life, we are
rewarded. Indeed, we find a glorious life that we couldn't attain on
our own.

If we want to be bigger than a mere existence, more than just a
being, and if we want to truly live, it can only be found in God. We
must continue on our hunt. Our pursuit of all that's good and true
must be an ongoing quest. It's like scoring the deal of a lifetime—an
eternal life in heaven where treasures abound!

Lord, I pray for your help in my pursuit of righteousness and
love. I want to find real life in you. Keep me on your path as I
continue my hunt.

ABUNDANT RAIN

Be glad, O children of Zion,
and rejoice in the LORD your God,
for he has given the early rain for your vindication;
he has poured down for you abundant rain,
the early and the latter rain, as before.

JOEL 2:23 ESV

Our Lord is so good and faithful. He provides us with everything we need if we only look to him for it. When our lives are in drought, parched from our daily grind, he sends us rain in abundance, to nourish our souls and keep us from drying out spiritually. The fields that are our lives begin to green up again after a season of becoming brown. We feel refreshed as his showers of love pour down over us.

Let's celebrate and be glad! Our God in heaven cares for us so much. He wants to see our trees bearing fruit, and he will continue to give us what we need to nourish and grow them. Turn to him when you are feeling parched, and he will give you rain.

Lord, thank you for protecting me from drying out. You give me everything I need to flourish, and for that I give you all the praise.

Rest Easy

Blessed be the Lord, who daily bears our burden,
The God who is our salvation.
   PSALM 68:19 NASB

There may be times when life's problems begin to feel overwhelming.
Do you know you can always rest in the knowledge that the Lord will
carry your burdens for you? He knows it all. He loves you. He is for you.
He saves you. He wants to rescue you. Allow him to do that for you.

Close your eyes and breathe in his presence. Permit him to come in
and take over every fiber of your being. Feel the Holy Spirit wash over
you, filling you up with his love. Then hand over each of your trials to
him, knowing that you cannot carry the load on your own. The Father
is strong enough to take them all. So let him.

Lord, thank you for being strong enough to carry the weight
of my burdens. I am amazed by your power and might! When
I am struggling, you are there to see me through. I know you
will rescue me when I am in need, and I praise you for it.

You Don't Have to Fight

In all these things we are more than conquerors through him who loved us.

ROMANS 8:37 NIV

Sit back for a moment and picture your troubles and hardships like a war. The battle is on, and you're slogging your way through it. You're fighting with all your might, just trying to keep up with the fray. Now imagine that a fearless leader is at the front line. He's slaying dragons left and right. This incredible warrior is knocking down every challenger. Anyone and everyone who dares to attack loses badly because of the skill in your commander. And in the end, you come out victorious, thanks to the one who leads you.

When we are on our own, every struggle and skirmish is exhausting, and it's a fight just to keep pace. But with God on our side, we become conquerors. Nothing can keep us down because the Lord's army is full of champions.

Father, thank you for fighting my battles for me. There is nothing that can overcome me with you by my side. I pray I would turn to you each time I struggle.

FAITHFUL WITHOUT FAIL

Let us hold firmly to the hope that we have confessed, because we can trust God to do what he promised.

HEBREWS 10:23 NCV

Did you know that the Lord is always faithful? He is! Always, without fail, he will follow through on what he tells us. Though there may be times when our earthly eyes have a hard time spotting him working in our day-to-day lives, he is always there. He has promised to be faithful to his children, and he will never go back on his Word.

So press on. Live in hope for your future and all the beauty that is ahead of you. Be confident in what he says. Hold on to your expectations for a life to come. Don't give in to the temptation to see only what's here and now. Keep your eyes on the future hope that eternal life provides.

Lord, I pray I'd keep my eyes fixed on you and the promises you have made. Sometimes I struggle to see past what's happening now. Help me to remember your Word, and see what's ahead. You have promised eternal life and a beautiful future, and I'm resting in that knowledge today. My hope is in you.

His Love Song

The LORD your God is in your midst,
a mighty one who will save;
he will rejoice over you with gladness;
he will quiet you by his love;
he will exult over you with loud singing.

ZEPHANIAH 3:17 ESV

One of the most popular reasons people buy puppies is so that there is always someone excited to see them when they get home. A puppy forgives quickly and loves to spend as much time with its owner as possible. But even better than the feeling you get from being with a dog is the delight that your Father in heaven takes in you. He actually rejoices over you and sings you a love song.

Smile! The Lord loves you fiercely. Our mighty warrior wants to save you from yourself. He gets great joy from his relationship with you. Join in his beautiful song and rejoice with him today.

Lord, thank you for loving me. I don't deserve it, but you take delight in me anyway. I pray I'd listen for your song with each and every waking moment, joining in the chorus and praising you all the while.

Intimate Friendship

The grace of the Lord Jesus Christ, and the love of God, and
the fellowship of the Holy Spirit, be with you all.
2 CORINTHIANS 13:14 NASB

What exactly does it mean to be in fellowship? It's a back-and-forth
relationship with shared interests. Most importantly, it's a friendship.
Isn't it amazing to know that the Holy Spirit himself wants this kind
of relationship with us? He is God, and we are certainly not. And yet,
he's looking for this connection with us.

God wants an intimate friendship with us: one where we really know
each other, where we go below surface level. His love is extravagant,
and he wants to lavish it on us as we look to him for relationship. No
matter what we do to mess it up, he wants to bring us back into the
fold and love on us for eternity. He is full of mercy and grace.

Lord, you consider me a friend, and it's simply extraordinary to
me. I pray I'd allow myself to go deeper with you today, and
find that intimate relationship that you crave with me. Thank
you for your extravagant love.

SHOUT HIS GOODNESS

Give thanks to the LORD and proclaim his greatness.
Let the whole world know what he has done.
Sing to him; yes, sing his praises.
Tell everyone about his wonderful deeds.
Exult in his holy name;
rejoice, you who worship the LORD.

1 CHRONICLES 16:8-10 NLT

When something great happens, sometimes we want to shout it on the mountain top, telling everyone who will listen. That's how we should feel about our relationship with Christ! By dying on the cross, taking away our sin, and loving us through our worst, he's done something incredible. We should be broadcasting it for all to hear.

God is the epitome of good. He has done so many wonderful things for us. Let's rejoice in that today, glorify his name to all who will listen, and praise him without ceasing. Revel in all his goodness.

Lord, thank you for all that you've done for me. My life would be nothing without you! I pray that I would be one who is willing to share your glory with those around me.

THE BEST OUTFIT

As God's chosen people, holy and dearly loved, clothe yourselves with compassion, kindness, humility, gentleness and patience.

COLOSSIANS 3:12 NIV

Women are known, in general, to be shoppers. They like thinking about what to wear, and they have a list of their go-to favorite items that make them feel good every time they put them on. But you know what always looks great? What always fits—no matter what time of the year it is? What never goes out of style? The list of attributes that mark us as Christians.

God asks us to clothe ourselves with compassion, kindness, humility, gentleness, and patience. These aren't always easy things to put on. Who really wants to wear humility? And sometimes it's just plain hard to wear patience. But when we remember to don these items, we'll always feel like we're wearing our finest.

Father, help me to remember to dress properly today, putting on the qualities that you desire for me. I pray others will see your love through me as I dress for the kingdom.

GROWING TRUST

I pray that Christ will be more and more at home in your hearts, living within you as you trust in him. May your roots go down deep into the soil of God's marvelous love; and may you be able to feel and understand, as all God's children should, how long, how wide, how deep, and how high his love really is.

EPHESIANS 3:17-19 TLB

Trusting the promises of God is a process that takes time. When you have a relationship with Jesus, the Holy Spirit dwells within you, guiding and encouraging you. As your relationship grows stronger, your love grows as well. With greater love comes greater trust as you see God's faithfulness day by day. As your trust grows, the roots of your faith will be built on his abounding love and perfect promises.

If you are struggling to trust God's faithfulness, begin reading his Word throughout the day. Speak to him, asking the Holy Spirit within you for guidance. Let his words of love be your constant companion and support.

Heavenly Father, I pray for a fuller understanding of your great love for me. I want to be consumed by your love and faithfulness, putting all my trust in you.

Ask Confidently

Let us come boldly to the very throne of God and stay there to receive his mercy and to find grace to help us in our times of need.

HEBREWS 4:16 TLB

It's hard to ask for help sometimes, isn't it? There's something truly humbling about admitting that we can't do everything on our own. When we let others know that we aren't as super human as we've been letting them believe, it's like a piece of us crumbles and our confidence drags. But in the kingdom of heaven, it's an entirely different story! We're told that we should hold our head up high when we ask for his help. He wants to give it, so approach him with joy and take the help he offers.

You are a precious child of God. He loves you deeply and wants the best for you. That means that it gives him joy to be able to help you in times of need. Swallow that pride and turn to him. You won't regret it!

Lord, thank you for your willingness to help me. I'm humbled by your grace, and I'm walking in confidence that I can approach you with my needs.

WILDEST DREAMS

To him who is able to do far more abundantly than all that we ask or think, according to the power at work within us, to him be glory in the church and in Christ Jesus throughout all generations, forever and ever.
EPHESIANS 3:20-21

Picture the greatest things you could ever imagine actually coming to fruition in your life. Your wildest dreams realized. Your greatest hopes come true. Guess what? It's all possible through our God. He can accomplish more than you could ever think to ask for. And you know what else is true? He wants to do it through you.

The Lord has given us the gift of the Holy Spirit living within us, guiding us, pressing us on toward achieving great things. He deserves all the glory and all the credit for the good we see around us. Let's praise him together and give him the honor. He is so good to us!

Father, you really are good. Thank you for using me as your tool to attain greatness for your kingdom. I know that I'm able to accomplish so much more with you than I ever could on my own.

VICTORY OVER STRUGGLES

How we thank God for all of this! It is he who makes us
victorious through Jesus Christ our Lord!

1 CORINTHIANS 15:57 TLB

If you are going through a battle today, take heart. Our God wants to
give you the victory over your struggles. Sin used to have destructive
power over your life, but no more. We are given freedom through
Jesus and the gift he gave us by dying on the cross.

No matter your burden, no matter your cares, look around and see
the joy that is ahead for you. It may feel like you are swimming
through peanut butter, trying to make it to the end of this trial, but
there is clear water ahead if you will just reach for it. Cast all of your
cares upon him, and he will relieve you of your burdens and claim
the victory for you. You'll triumph over every difficulty because he is
leading the charge against the attack.

Father, thank you for giving me victory over the assaults
coming at me. Sin has no power over me. I'm amazed at your
gift of Jesus Christ and in awe of the strength you've given me
because of him.

EFFORTLESSLY GOOD

The LORD is good;
his steadfast love endures forever,
and his faithfulness to all generations.
PSALM 100:5 ESV

The Lord is good, always and forever. The list of ways in which he loves us is endless. Every day there is reason to rejoice because we serve a God who is the very essence of good. Have you ever tried to be good, all the time? It's an impossible task for us. But God makes it look easy, and it truly is for him.

Our good, good God loves us so much and tells us so hundreds of times throughout the pages of the Bible. He forgives us over and over again. He shows us mercy and grace. His goodness will stand the test of time and last forevermore throughout the ages. It's a promise we can count on. His Word says that his faithfulness will continue through all generations.

Father, I am amazed by who you are. You are effortlessly good, and I am thankful to be a recipient of your everlasting love and mercy. I pray I'd remember your enduring love each time I begin to falter or doubt you.

STAND YOUR GROUND

Stand firm. Let nothing move you. Always give yourselves fully to the work of the Lord, because you know that your labor in the Lord is not in vain.

1 CORINTHIANS 15:58 NIV

There are times in which we all grow weary. It can be hard to live for the kingdom, following the straight and narrow path we're called to walk on. But we are told to stand firm, to stand our ground. There is a reward coming that is greater than anything you can imagine. It's worth the work and the extra effort!

Take a deep breath. Breathe in his life and his love today. He will give you what you need to continue on your path. Your labor is not in vain, and it doesn't go unnoticed. Unspeakable joy is your gift for the taking. Be confident that nothing you do or say for his glory is a waste of time or energy.

Lord, I am confident in what I do because you give me joy. Thank you for loving me through the hard days. I pray that I'd sense your presence at every turn and through every difficulty.

You Can Always Pray

I urge you, first of all, to pray for all people. Ask God to help them; intercede on their behalf, and give thanks for them. Pray this way for kings and all who are in authority so that we can live peaceful and quiet lives marked by godliness and dignity.

1 TIMOTHY 2:1-2 NLT

Ever feel like your hands are tied and there's just nothing you can do about a certain situation? Rest assured; that is never the case. You can always pray. In fact, we are encouraged to pray about every situation, in every way we know how. We are even told to pray for our country's leaders even when we don't agree with the decisions they make.

Daily conversation with the Lord is the key to living a joy-filled life. Lifting others up, interceding for them, and giving God thanks are all a huge part of the regular discussions we should be having. When you feel as if there is nothing you can do, stop everything and begin to pray.

Father, thank you for listening to me when I pray. You deserve all the praise and glory for answering prayer the way you do even when it's not the way I had hoped for. Our conversations give me joy!

YOUR THOUGHT LIFE

Letting your sinful nature control your mind leads to death. But letting the Spirit control your mind leads to life and peace.

ROMANS 8:6 NLT

Thoughts are more powerful than we give them credit. Actions always start with a thought. Good actions, God-honoring actions, happen because they were first a thought in someone's mind. Bad actions are also a direct response to thoughts. This is why it's critical to pay attention to your thought life.

Problems present themselves when, try as you might, you can't seem to control your thought life. Do self-destructive thoughts often arise in your mind? There is great news for you today. You are too weak to make any changes on your own. But the Spirit of Christ that dwells within you has all the power you need.

Father, thank you that your Spirit brings life and peace. Please fill me with more of your Spirit today that my mind might be more at peace.

THE TIME OF DAY

This is what the LORD says—the LORD who made the earth, who formed and established it, whose name is the LORD: "Ask me and I will tell you remarkable secrets you do not know about things to come."
JEREMIAH 33:2-3

Isn't it comforting to know that the Lord is our friend? Like someone who is just a phone call away, he's always willing to listen to us. He tells us that if we call to him, he will answer us. Not only that, but he's going to give us the lowdown on great things that we would never otherwise know. Isn't it amazing?

He is God, and we are not; yet, he still gives us the time of day—each and every day! So when you're weary, when you're worried, when you're stressed and feeling blue, call out to him. Ask him for what you need, and he will provide you with incredible wisdom.

Father, I'm calling out to you today. I'm asking for help and for your love and peace to wash down over me in this moment. May I feel that peace throughout this day, and continue to soak it in.

APRIL

"If you sinful people know how to give good gifts to your children, how much more will your heavenly Father give good gifts to those who ask him."

MATTHEW 7:11 NLT

MADE WHOLE

May the God of peace himself sanctify you completely, and may your whole spirit and soul and body be kept blameless at the coming of our Lord Jesus Christ.

1 THESSALONIANS 5:23 ESV

We are made up of three parts: body, soul, and spirit. Our body and soul are constantly battling against temptation and our earthly desires. But our spirit? That's where the Lord himself lives within us. We might ask ourselves why we deserve his great love for us, and the truth is that we don't. God looks at us and sees perfection because he is in us.

God takes all of our broken pieces, fits them back together, and makes us healthy and whole. We are able to be blameless at the end of our days simply because he enters in and fixes us. We should rejoice at this! He takes one look at us and determines that we are worthy, and it's all because of him.

Father, thank you for fixing me. I pray that I'd allow you in, fully and completely, to do the work in me that you need to do. I'm grateful for your love.

WORTH WORRYING ABOUT

There is only one thing worth being concerned about. Mary
has discovered it, and it will not be taken away from her.
LUKE 10:42 NLT

Have you ever left a dinner party only to realize you barely spoke two
words to the hostess? Maybe you've *been* that hostess. The food was
probably fantastic, but now you need to schedule a host of coffee
dates to actually connect with your friends.

The familiar Bible story of Mary and Martha is so well-known mostly
because it's an invaluable lesson. If we are not mindful, anxiety over
details and particulars can take over our lives, robbing us of the
things that are actually worth worrying about, like fellowship, truth,
and seeking God's face.

Jesus, thank you for this timeless reminder today. As worry and
anxiety threaten to distract me, may I be found at your feet,
taking in your presence.

LIGHT OF LOVE

You are a chosen people, royal priests, a holy nation, a people for God's own possession. You were chosen to tell about the wonderful acts of God, who called you out of darkness into his wonderful light.

1 PETER 2:9 NCV

Whenever you start to doubt the love that God has for you, simply turn to his Word and be reminded of the truth. He picked you! He chose you as his special possession. He wants a relationship with you, and he wants you to work with him to draw others into the light of his kingdom.

Before we knew Jesus as our Savior, we lived in darkness. Now life is bright! Jesus is the lamp that illuminates the path ahead of us, directing us where to go, and what to say and do. Let's declare his praises together, and stay in the brilliance of his light.

Lord, thank you for choosing me as your special possession. I can scarcely believe that you'd want me, but I'm so grateful that you do! My darkness has gone, and I want to live only in the light of your love.

No Need to Fear

Now this is what the Lord says.
He created you, people of Jacob;
he formed you, people of Israel.
He says, "Don't be afraid, because I have saved you.
I have called you by name, and you are mine."

ISAIAH 43:1 NCV

Over and over again, throughout the pages of the Bible, we are told not to have fear. The reason is simple. The Lord has redeemed us. There is nothing that can take us down from this point on. He took us in the palm of his hand, and he said to himself, "This one is mine. This one belongs to me."

He has saved us from ourselves, and has made atonement for our sins by dying on the cross. There is no better or bigger gift. It means we don't have to worry for the future or be afraid to see what it holds. We know beauty, grace, love, mercy, and eternal life are in store for us.

Lord, I'm so glad I belong to you and no other. Thank you for redeeming me from the life I would have chosen for myself. I look forward to my future because you are in it!

STEPPING OUT

The Spirit God gave us does not make us timid, but gives us power, love and self-discipline.

2 TIMOTHY 1:7 NIV

When the Holy Spirit begins to dwell in us, we are changed in many incredible ways. Because of his power within us, we can't play the shrinking violet card any more. We're not wallflowers; we're children of God! The life of his party! When our own spirit feels too timid to speak boldly, the Holy Spirit steps in for us and gives us courage.

There's a fire ablaze within you. Keep it going by stepping out in new ways. You can do it! God believes in you. Take risks for him, and be confident and courageous. The Holy Spirit is with you every step of the way.

Lord, thank you for sending me your Holy Spirit to dwell within me and guide me. Give me courage to share your love with others. Help me to lose my timidity and gain your power.

FAITHFUL IN PRAYER

Rejoice in our confident hope. Be patient in trouble, and keep on praying.

ROMANS 12:12 NLT

It can be difficult to keep joy alive as you wait expectantly for something big to happen. And patience? That is tough for just about everyone. The good news is that we don't have to make it happen on our own. The Holy Spirit provides joy that surpasses any emotion we would otherwise experience on our own. When we ask him for patience, it will come. When we are tempted to give up, we need to pray even harder.

Through the worst of times, there is joy to be found. We are loved beyond measure by our Creator, and though our afflictions may threaten to pull us down, if we cast our cares on him, he will be there to support us. All we need to do is be faithful in prayer, turning to him for every need and with each cry of our hearts.

Lord, it's amazing what I can do when I do it with you. Joy and patience abound in me because you have changed my heart.

PRAISE HIM

I will praise you with an upright heart,
when I learn your righteous rules.
PSALM 119:7 ESV

The Lord is deserving of so much praise. There is nothing we have that he hasn't provided for us. Doesn't it make your heart sing to think of all of his wonderful ways? He is so good to us. If we live by his law, and make the choice to follow him, we can praise him with an unburdened, pure heart.

It is a choice, isn't it? He doesn't force us into loving him. Instead, our God leaves it up to us. We can opt to walk away, to follow our own path and forge our own way. Alone, afraid, and unsure, we can blaze a trail of our own. Or we can look to him to find righteousness, joy, and life. Let's choose him! It will be the best choice we could ever make.

Father, I choose you! I praise you today because you are worthy of all the glory and honor. Thank you for providing your Word and your laws as a roadmap to living a righteous life. You are such a good God.

No Grudges

Be kind to each other, tenderhearted, forgiving one another, just as God has forgiven you because you belong to Christ.

EPHESIANS 4:32 TLB

If ever there was a verse to read daily, it's this one. Who couldn't use a little more kindness and compassion in their lives? Each day, we come up against human frailty. We are hurt by the people we allow into our lives simply because people are far from perfect. They're bound to make mistakes. Instead of holding a grudge, and keeping a tight grip on our list of grievances, we can make a clean break and release it to God.

Christ died so that we could be forgiven. He deals with us gently and mercifully. Because we are made in his image, we need to turn that grace around and direct it toward those we love. Let's choose kindness. It's amazing how our own hearts are changed when we choose to be compassionate to others.

Lord, thank you for forgiving me for my many sins. I pray you'd help me to show kindness and compassion toward others, truly forgiving them when they hurt me.

MUCH STRONGER

Be strong in the Lord and in his mighty power.
EPHESIANS 6:10 NIV

You have a strength you may not know you possess. Sure, there are days when it's a battle just to get up, when it seems like the world is pitted against you and you're not certain you'll be able to fight your way through. But you've got a secret power. It's called the Holy Spirit, and he's ready to give you his strength when you no longer have any of your own.

Thank goodness we don't have to stand in our own power. How exhausting it would be, slogging through the daily grind by ourselves. On our own, we are repetitively lifting those puny one-pound weights, going nowhere. But with Christ, we become Olympic-ready weight lifters, throwing a heavier load on each time and hardly exerting ourselves. God is mighty, and he gladly shares his strength with us.

Lord, I'm in awe of your power and might. I'm so thankful that you make me strong—so much stronger than I am on my own!

WORKING WITH JOY

Whatever you do, do your work heartily, as for the Lord rather than for men, knowing that from the Lord you will receive the reward of the inheritance. It is the Lord Christ whom you serve.

COLOSSIANS 3:23-24 NASB

We are each called to do different work, whether it's behind a desk, caring for children, cleaning a home, or selling products. Sometimes the daily grind of work can be exhausting. You may not want to work wholeheartedly. Perhaps you just want to get through the day and be done. But when you serve a heavenly master, there's a greater reward than a paycheck waiting for you. We are promised an inheritance that's better than anything we can imagine.

Let's put our minds to working with joy. Let's work with thankful servant hearts, knowing that our effort is seen and appreciated, and that we are serving one who loves us beyond comparison. You'll be surprised at how this mindset switch can change your life.

Lord, I want to serve you! I'm excited to receive my inheritance from you. Help me to put my efforts into working with my whole heart while I wait for my reward.

THE ROCK

Trust in the LORD always,
for the LORD GOD is the eternal Rock.
ISAIAH 26:4 NLT

What do you think of when you think of a rock? Do you think of words like solid, strong, and firm? These words are just a few of the fitting descriptors we can use when we talk about our God. He is solid and dependable. He is more than strong enough for you. He is the firm foundation on which you can build your future.

It's easy to trust someone who is solid, right? You know they'll be there for you, and that they won't crumble under pressure. That's our God! Smile. Relax. Breathe deeply, and be secure in the knowledge that he is your rock today, tomorrow, and forever. He will never let you down. You no longer have to worry or live in fear because you've got a firm foundation to stand upon.

Lord, thank you for being my rock. I cannot imagine life without you. I give myself over to you, trusting in you completely because I know that you won't let me down, from here to eternity.

Prone to Wander

May the Lord lead your hearts into God's love
and Christ's patience.

2 THESSALONIANS 3:5 NCV

Our hearts are prone to wandering, aren't they? Our humanity gets
in the way of our best intentions, and we often struggle to stay the
course. But the Lord can work any miracle. He raised people from the
dead and healed the sick. Surely he can take your heart and direct
you back toward love when you stray! He will take you by the hand
and lead you right to where you belong—to the path of God's great
love and Christ's endurance.

We can do anything we want when we do it alongside our God. More
than anything, we should want to do life as he's asked it of us. We
should desire to live with love. Let's give our God the praise for being
our teacher of all that's good and our director in life. We know that
we can make wise choices for our hearts because he shows us the way
and gives us the power to choose well.

Lord, thank you for guiding me to the path you want for me.
I pray I'd turn to you each time I'm tempted to stray.

GREAT BONUS

You have need of endurance, so that when you have done the will of God you may receive what is promised.

HEBREWS 10:36 ESV

What does it mean to persevere? It means that we continue in a course of action even in the face of difficulty or with little or no prospect of success. You push on when the going gets tough, and stand against opponents that come your way. That's what we are called to do. The good news is that it isn't all for naught. There's a reward coming for us. God has promised life eternal in heaven, and that's a pretty good bonus for a life of work.

So when you are tempted to stray from God's plan for you, remember his promises and stick it out. He wants you to reap that reward. Allow him to work in you so that you can be there to accept it. It'll be the best payment for work you'll ever receive.

Lord, thank you for your promises. I can't wait to receive your gift of eternal life. Help me to persevere in the work that you have for me, today and every day.

REFRESHMENT SOURCE

O God, You are my God; I shall seek You earnestly;
My soul thirsts for You, my flesh yearns for You,
In a dry and weary land where there is no water.

PSALM 63:1 NASB

When we are thirsty, our body lets us know. If we go too long without quenching our thirst, we slowly begin to shut down. We don't function properly. Our thirst is at the forefront of our mind, and we wonder when we are going to get something to satisfy our need.

This is how we should feel when we go too long without daily conversations with the Lord. We should feel as if we just can't function properly because a vital part of what we need to fuel ourselves is missing from our system. Thankfully, we don't have to thirst for long. The Lord is available to us whenever we need him. The landscape of our lives need never feel like a desert. We can simply turn to him, and drink in his love. It's a never-ending source of refreshment.

Father, I thirst for you. Fill me up with your living water today, refreshing my soul and satisfying every part of me.

NOTHING HIDDEN

There is no creature hidden from His sight, but all things are open and laid bare to the eyes of Him with whom we have to do.
HEBREWS 4:13 NASB

There is nothing we can do that is hidden from God. While at times that knowledge may make us squirm (after all, we are far from perfect, and there are things we'd just rather keep tucked away), it really should be comforting. He sees it all, and he loves us anyway! God knows the worst of what we've got going on, and he continues on in his pursuit of our hearts.

There is nothing we can do to make him stop loving us. Yes, we are held accountable. Yes, he knows when we fall short. But despite our flaws, and regardless of our circumstances, he takes us by the hand, and he loves unconditionally. Rejoice in the knowledge that you cannot keep secrets from your heavenly Father. It's freeing to know the he sees all and still chooses love.

Lord, thank you for knowing me intimately. You know my flaws and love me despite them. I am humbled by who you are.

INTIMATELY FASHIONED

The Lord looks from heaven;
He sees all the sons of men.
From the place of His dwelling He looks
On all the inhabitants of the earth;
He fashions their hearts individually;
He considers all their works.

PSALM 33:13-15 NKJV

Don't you love how the Lord knows us so intimately? He formed our very hearts. God molded us, shaped us, and created us. He watches over us from heaven. There is nothing we do that we do alone. We take no step on our own. He is always with us. Whenever we feel lost or lonely, we can take refuge in the knowledge that he will never leave those he created.

God knows what we will say before we say it, what we will think before we think it, and what we will do before we do it. He watches in delight when we choose well and with concern when we don't. But he never walks away, and never forsakes us. Our Father is always there for us, cheering us on.

Thank you for watching over me, Lord. I'm so comforted by the knowledge that you will never leave me, no matter what.

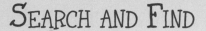

SEARCH AND FIND

You will also begin to search again for Jehovah your God, and
you will find him when you search for him with all your heart
and soul.

DEUTERONOMY 4:29 TLB

There is nothing more that the Lord wants from us than to draw
deeper together in relationship with him. He knows that we are at our
best when we are walking closely with him. He doesn't hide from us.
He doesn't make it difficult for us to find him. We simply have to seek
the Lord and he will reveal himself to us.

God makes it so easy for us. He offers his love on a silver platter, as
a gift, if we will only make the effort to open our hearts and eyes to
him. And it feels so good when we do. Together, let's be at our best,
seeking him daily with all our hearts and with all of our souls.

Father, thank you for making it so easy to find love with you!
Reveal yourself to me. I'm ready to seek you, and to discover
all that you have to offer.

A BEAUTIFUL SOUND

To choose life is to love the LORD your God, obey him, and stay
close to him. He is your life, and he will let you live many
years in the land, the land he promised to give your ancestors
Abraham, Isaac, and Jacob.

DEUTERONOMY 30:20 NCV

We were created to love hearing beautiful things. We listen to music,
we smile at the sound of children's laughter, and the birds chirping
on a crisp spring morning is a sweet melody to our ears. But the most
beautiful sound of all is the sound of the Lord's voice speaking to
us. We can hear him if we listen. And when we choose to obey his
teachings and cling to him, it's an incredible song of joy to our Savior.

God is life. He is the source of everything. Let's sing with him
together, a new song of redemption and love, for all who have ears
to hear. Listen for his voice. He is calling to you! It's a sound of pure
beauty.

Father, thank you for your voice. I pray I will choose to obey
you when you call to me, and hold fast to your teachings.

LIVING ABUNDANTLY

The thief comes only to steal and kill and destroy; I have come that they may have life, and have it to the full.

JOHN 10:10 NIV

At the end of a great story, the good guy comes out a victor, triumphing over the villain. Welcome to real life as a Christian! There's a villain in the story of our lives, but with Christ we defeat him every day. A would-be thief, the devil himself, wants to destroy us, but God isn't willing to let that happen. Instead, he wants us to live abundant lives.

Living abundantly means to have overflow, excess, over-and-above, profit, surplus, and more-than-sufficient love. It fills us up and flows out of us, spilling onto others. God wants our entire body, soul, and spirit to be full of him and the blessing that his love brings. He is the hero of our life's story. Let's give him all the praise and credit he deserves!

Lord, you are my hero. Each and every day, you rescue me. Thank you for filling me to the brim with your love and claiming victory over the enemy.

AGAPE LOVE

We love because he first loved us.
1 JOHN 4:19 ESV

God loves you. It's a simple statement, but it's a powerful one. God doesn't just love you. He loves you with *agape* love. What does that mean? It means that he chooses to love you. Agape love is love of will rather than emotion. It's a love that always seeks the highest good, no matter what others do. It's an unconditional love, and it's what God feels for you.

Can you imagine? God doesn't just love you because he's a good God and he has to. He chooses you every day. The Lord says, "Yep, she just fell short of perfection again. She did exactly what I told her not to do. But I will love her through it. I will lift her up, dust her off, and set her back on her feet." He has chosen you. Now you get to choose to love him right back!

Father, thank you for your agape love—for choosing to love me. I choose to love you today with all of my heart.

FEAST OF LOVE

O taste and see that the LORD is good;
How blessed is the man who takes refuge in Him!
PSALM 34:8 NASB

Let's be honest, there's not much that's better than a delicious meal. Close your eyes and picture your favorite foods all laid out on a table before you. What would be there? A juicy steak? Creamy pasta? A sushi platter? Whatever your options would be, they are nothing compared to the feast of love that a relationship with the Lord has for you. It tastes better than anything you've ever known.

The best part is that you can indulge whenever you want, any time—day or night. It's calorie free, and it's good for you. So go ahead; taste and see that the Lord is good. He's the best, and he wants to share all that he has with you.

Lord, I want to taste all that you desire for me. Let me share in your feast of heavenly goodness, desiring you above all else and taking refuge in your love. Thank you for your generosity.

PLACE YOUR HOPE IN GOD

Guide me in your truth and teach me,
for you are God my Savior,
and my hope is in you all day long.
PSALM 25:5 NIV

When you are at your wit's end, who do you look to for help? If you are putting your hope in God, then you will never be let down. When you hang onto his truth and allow him to teach you, it's easy to put your hope in him. And when you accept Christ as your Savior, he lives in you each day and stokes the fire in your soul, keeping hope alive in your body and spirit.

You have hope for a future, because he is your past, your present, and your everything from here on out. Put all your hope in him, and you will see the reward.

Lord, I'm putting my hope and trust in you. Guide me in your truth. Teach me your ways. You are my Savior and I'm so thankful for that!

CROWNED WITH LOVE

Let all that I am praise the LORD;
with my whole heart, I will praise his holy name.
Let all that I am praise the LORD;
may I never forget the good things he does for me.
He forgives all my sins
and heals all my diseases.
He redeems me from death
and crowns me with love and tender mercies.
He fills my life with good things.
My youth is renewed like the eagle's!

PSALM 103:1-5 NLT

Everything we have is a gift from God. We would be nowhere without him. Nope, scratch that. We would be in the muck and mire, for all eternity, without him. But he has pulled us out of our hopelessness. He took one look at our sorry selves and crowned us with love and compassion.

Let's praise him all the days of our lives. Let's raise our voices to the heavens and worship him. God has forgiven our sins so we can live with unending and abundant joy.

Father, thank you for your forgiving heart. I give you all the praises, because it is from you alone that all good things flow.

FORGOTTEN FAILURE

I will forgive their wickedness
and will remember their sins no more.
HEBREWS 8:12 NIV

It is so hard to forget when someone has done us wrong. We've got long memories when it comes to the injustices we see in our lives. But thank goodness that's not how the Lord operates! His loving heart forgives us in his mercy. When we are repentant, he forgives us and wipes our slates clean. There's no holding on to the list of our failings for future reference. Instead it's as if it never happened.

What freedom we have knowing that we can unburden ourselves from the guilt of past wrong doings. There is no need to punish ourselves over and over again; if we have gone to him with remorse, he has forgiven and forgotten.

Lord, thank you for forgiving me of my sins. I praise you even more for forgetting them entirely, wiping them from my history. I am constantly amazed by who you are.

A Peaceful Place

Then Jesus said, "Let's go off by ourselves to a quiet place and rest awhile." He said this because there were so many people coming and going that Jesus and his apostles didn't even have time to eat.

MARK 6:31 NLT

Life gets crowded sometimes. It's not always easy to get away from the things that cause our anxiety—endless to-do lists, busy holidays, visits from family, work deadlines—life gets hectic and stress builds up. Jesus shows us that there is a time and a place for refreshing. Like the disciples, we can and should *go off by ourselves to a quiet place and rest awhile.*

When life's troubles begin to press in, take Jesus' advice. If only for half an hour, spend time in prayer, or read his Word, or sing his praises. Acts of worship can bring the release from stress and anxiety that we so desperately need.

Jesus, you truly know my anxieties. Show me a peaceful place and meet with me there. Calm my anxious heart and give me your quiet rest.

QUIET BEAUTY

Your beauty should come from within you—the beauty of a gentle and quiet spirit that will never be destroyed and is very precious to God.

1 PETER 3:4 NCV

Let's say a prayer of thanks that God sees our inner beauty and not just what we see in the mirror. Scars, wrinkles, droops, and stretched skin are invisible to his searching eye, but beautiful hearts are fully exposed. While some enjoy the advantages of outer beauty in this world, those with a gentle and quiet spirit will be rejoicing in the kingdom of heaven.

If you're nervous that your inner beauty doesn't measure up to his gaze, take heart. The more time you spend with Jesus, the more you will come to look, sound, and act like him. You reflect his character more and more with each passing day spent in his presence.

Jesus, let your beauty shine through me. Let the darkness of my inner heart be filled with the light of your glory as I reflect the gentle and quiet beauty that is so precious to you.

JOY IS A CHOICE

This is the day the LORD has made.
We will rejoice and be glad in it.
PSALM 118:24 NLT

It's fair to say that some days are harder than others. Some days the sun doesn't shine, the day ahead feels daunting, and it seems almost impossible to rise out of bed. Thankfully the joy that God has rooted into our hearts is not circumstantial.

Joy is not dependent on our financial situation, our relationships with others, or our emotional state. It may take some effort, but it is his joy that calls us out of our hiding places. It is what allows us to see the beauty in the midst of chaos and turmoil. It is what causes us to rejoice, and praise him, even if the floor beneath us seems to be crumbling. Joy is a choice—a gift to embrace daily. In every situation, good or bad, God has given it to us for the taking.

God, thank you that every day from you is a precious gift. Lord, help me see your joy in everything I encounter today. Help me see your unfailing goodness in every situation. Let your joy be rooted in my spirit.

LASTING COMFORT

If the LORD had not been my help,
my soul would soon have lived in the land of silence.
When I thought, "My foot is slipping,"
your steadfast love, O LORD, held me up.

PSALM 94:17-18 NRSV

Whether we need comforting or are offering comfort to a friend, ultimately our highest peace will come from the presence of God. A shoulder to cry on, a warm cup of tea, a good strong hug...each might help ease the pain for a short while. But these are merely short-term gifts offered from human hands. We need God's presence—not temporary presents—to truly relax our minds and hearts.

When God comes to us, he strengthens us not with fleeting things we may want or desire, but with his unfailing love and support. His comfort is everlasting and it strengthens us for the road ahead.

O Lord, you know my needs and my wants. Help me seek your eternal comfort and not the comfort of worldly things. Strengthen me in my weakness, supporting me and renewing me in your love!

More than Seasonal Compassion

He will rescue the poor when they cry to him;
he will help the oppressed, who have no one to defend them.
He feels pity for the weak and the needy, and he will rescue them.
He will redeem them from oppression and violence,
for their lives are precious to him.

PSALM 72:12-14 NLT

It can be impossible to find a food shelf or homeless shelter in need of volunteers during the holidays when people are more likely to think about the welfare of others. We become acutely compassionate that time of year and our eyes and hearts are more fully open to the love our Savior showed us when he came as a baby, needy and poor. Our hearts are moved to bestow that same love wherever we can. God rejoices in our giving, as do the recipients of the gift, but are we faithful to this call to compassion every season of the year?

God sees the unloved, rejected, and defenseless *every day*. He comforts the weak and violated in the depths of their wretchedness regardless of season. His compassion is not waiting for a holiday, and he needs no excuse to shower it over anyone who cries out to him. As his hands and feet, are you bringing his words of help and redemption to the precious lives of the oppressed?

Heavenly Father, keep my eyes open every day of the year to see the unloved and the burdened, that I may show them your love and your strength that can shoulder their troubles. I welcome opportunities to put your compassion into action.

DEEPEST CONTENTMENT

He will keep in perfect peace all those who trust in him, whose thoughts turn often to the Lord!

ISAIAH 26:3 TLB

When we put our trust in God, and only in God, we find a peace that truly satisfies our distress. Scripture repeatedly advises us to keep our thoughts on the Lord, with our eyes focused on his promises, because it is in God that our deepest contentment and joy are found. We can search our whole lives for pleasures, wealth, and success in the hope that peace and fulfillment will come, but only an intimate relationship with God can give us that.

Where are you looking for your contentment? Is true peace eluding you? The more we focus on ourselves, the more peace eludes us. But the more we focus on God, the more his peace sustains us.

God, you are faithful to meet all of my needs. Help me to focus my thoughts on you because the world has nothing for me! Only in Jesus, whose love and faithfulness never cease, will I find peace.

MAY

You, Lord, are forgiving and good,
abounding in love to all who call on you.

PSALM 86:5 NIV

For Us, Not Against Us

What, then, shall we say in response to these things? If God is for us, who can be against us?

ROMANS 8:31 NIV

God is for us. What a powerful idea that the God of the universe is *for* us. We sometimes buy into this untruthful image of God, depicting him as angry, distant, and condemning. But God is for us; he is not against us. His heart toward us has eternally been compassionate, loving, merciful, and tender.

God's desire for unhindered relationship with us is displayed impeccably by Christ—who laid everything down to fight for our hearts.

Heavenly Father, I pray that whenever I begin to feel as though you are against me, I would remember that it is the opposite that's true. You have been for me since the beginning. You are not against me; you are my friend. Thank you for your steadfast love and your unfailing mercy.

In the Darkness

The LORD is close to the brokenhearted,
and he saves those whose spirits have been crushed.

PSALM 34:18 NCV

Jesus was a man of great sorrow, acquainted with bitter grief. He was mocked and despised, rejected and abused. He understands our depression and relates personally to our pain. If you feel that all strength and hope have gone, Jesus knows the dark depths of your grief. His heart breaks with yours, and he has promised to save you!

If you're feeling depressed, healing can begin by regaining a godly perspective. Reconnect with your heavenly Father, seeking his purpose for your life. Sometimes rest, healthy nutrition, and time alone with God are enough to illuminate a path shadowed in darkness. If not, a godly counselor can help shed light and gain the perspective that has been lost. Above all, know that you are never alone; God is always close to you and has never left your side.

Heavenly Father, you know me, my heart, and my sorrows. I'm reaching out to you with the little strength I have, grasping for the One who promises to save those whose spirits have been crushed. Save me, O God, as only one close to heartbreak can.

THE LIFELINE

All need to be made right with God by his grace, which is a free gift. They need to be made free from sin through Jesus Christ. God sent him to die in our place to take away our sins. We receive forgiveness through faith in the blood of Jesus' death.

ROMANS 3:24-25 NCV

While life can seem to be increasingly complicated and turbulent, faith remains simple. It is our lifeline to God, who brings all things under his control. While sin breaks our connection to God, the act of faith in Jesus Christ and the repentance from sin make us right with God. When we put our faith in Jesus, God no longer sees our sin, as if the line had never been broken at all.

What troubles can overwhelm us when our lifeline runs straight to the Creator of heaven and earth? When your faith is rooted and established in Jesus, you have everything you need.

Gracious God, thank you that you have given the free gift of salvation through Jesus Christ. By faith, I can draw near to you and trust you. I am free of guilt and can walk with confidence, no matter the circumstances.

WHITE AS WOOL

Come, let's talk this over, says the Lord; no matter how deep the stain of your sins, I can take it out and make you as clean as freshly fallen snow. Even if you are stained as red as crimson, I can make you white as wool!

ISAIAH 1:18 TLB

The Lord knows that his promise of complete forgiveness is hard for us to believe. So he's willing to discuss it. It's going to need some talking over before our human hearts can really let the truth sink in: *we are fully, completely, totally forgiven.* No matter how shameful, depraved, or evil the sins of our past, *he has wiped them clean.* He has taken the stain out, though it was deep and dark. Though we were red as crimson, now we are white as wool.

It's a remarkably beautiful image. If you have repented of sin and asked for forgiveness, you are perfectly pure. If not, don't wait another moment! Talk it over with God, who has all the time you need. All you have to do is ask.

Thank you, God, that your forgiveness is complete! Help me to see myself the way you see me: white as wool and fully forgiven.

SET FREE!

Live as free people, but do not use your freedom as an excuse to do evil. Live as servants of God.

1 PETER 2:16 NCV

When a prisoner is set free, it is with the expectation that their criminal acts are a thing of the past. When we are set free in Christ, God's expectation is that we will put our sinful deeds behind us and live in service to him. Because of our freedom, we are no longer subject to the bonds of guilt, sin, and fear. Instead, we are free to walk in the grace, redemption, and joy that abound in the life of one serving Jesus.

Sin can continue to plague believers even as they draw near to God. Often it is because the love for God is deepening that Satan's attacks persist. Take a stand against the enemy with prayer and God's Word, fighting for freedom with Jesus at your side. You are not a slave; you are set free!

Thank you, Jesus, for setting me free from sin! My mind and heart are renewed as I live to worship and serve you with my life. Strengthen me to stand against any sin that would draw me back to slavery.

FRIENDS IN THE FIGHT

As iron sharpens iron,
so people can improve each other.
PROVERBS 27:17 NCV

Friends are one of life's greatest joys; laughter and tears are both shared around the love-worn tables of true friends. Without them, life can seem empty and lonely. Friends are marked by their loyalty, love, and perhaps most importantly, their honesty. A friend is by your side, confronting the harsh trials of life with honest insight and godly counsel, even if the truth is difficult or painful. God uses our friends to strengthen us.

Some of us may be surrounded by true friends, while others have only a couple at their side. Regardless of the size of your army, you are made powerful by your common loyalty to God. Standing together, friends unified by Christ can overcome anything.

Sharpen me, O Lord, and the friends around me, so that we may fight the good fight of faith together. Give us humble hearts to hear your truth. And let prayer and your Word be the ties that bind our friendships, no matter what joys or troubles life may bring.

A Beautiful Day

I will recount the steadfast love of the LORD,
the praises of the LORD,
according to all that the LORD has granted us,
and the great goodness to the house of Israel
that he has granted them according to his compassion,
according to the abundance of his steadfast love.

ISAIAH 63:7 ESV

We can claim the truth of this verse each and every day, regardless of our circumstances or emotions. His goodness is great every day; his steadfast love is abundant. We can show God how thankful we are by remembering his goodness and telling others all that he has done for us.

God's goodness never waivers and his love for you never decreases. Even if life seems like drudgery and today feels rotten to the core, the list of blessings in your life is quite long. Recall the steadfast love he has granted to you, his goodness and compassion, and know that according to them, this day is beautiful.

You are so good, God! Your goodness cannot be recounted in one day alone, but I will rejoice in attempting to remember as many blessings as I can. Thank you for your steadfast love and compassion.

GLORIOUS CYCLE

All of this is for your benefit. And as God's grace reaches more and more people, there will be great thanksgiving, and God will receive more and more glory.

2 CORINTHIANS 4:15 NLT

What a beautiful picture: when we are given grace, we feel God's love and can't wait to share it with others. They then share our excitement and also give thanks to God, who receives the glory he rightly deserves. The more we glorify him, the more his grace is exalted and shared, and the glorious cycle continues.

It begins with God's grace: the simple yet astounding gift of God's favor. We cannot earn it and we don't deserve it, but it pours out abundantly over us purely because God loves us. Grace changes us, transforming our countenance to shine more like the face of Jesus. We shine on the lost and broken-hearted, spreading God's grace where it's needed most. Glory to God!

Gracious God, your gifts overflow in my life! I pour out my thanksgiving to you, O Lord, and ask for my testimony to reach more and more people. May your grace be glorified!

FULL OF GUIDANCE

Trust in the LORD with all your heart;
do not depend on your own understanding.
Seek his will in all you do,
and he will show you which path to take.
Don't be impressed with your own wisdom.
Instead fear the LORD and turn away from evil.

PROVERBS 3:5-7 NLT

God's Word is full of guidance. If we are faithful to seek his good advice and are dedicated to following it, we can make choices that are wise and pleasing to him. If a difficult decision is plaguing you, know that God isn't hiding the answers. He wants to guide you in the right path. He doesn't keep his will for you a secret; he will share his help when you ask.

Quiet the noise in your life, and listen to God's Word. He will speak to you, and as you walk closer with him each day, you will come to understand his voice.

Heavenly Father, I need your guidance. Calm my mind and heart so that I can listen to your voice. Help me to obediently walk in your will every day, giving me the strength I need.

ALL PROMISES KEPT

Through Christ you believe in God, who raised Christ from the dead and gave him glory. So your faith and your hope are in God.
1 PETER 1:21 NCV

We can confidently put our hope in God because all of his promises are true. When we stop believing that he is faithful, we stop having hope. But the resurrection of Jesus Christ after his death on the cross is the foundation of our hope. Jesus promised that he would rise from the dead, and he did. Now we can know that every other promise he makes is also true.

Have you given up hope? Perhaps the promises you have been waiting for have remained unfulfilled. Remember these promises and know that God is loving and gracious; according to his perfect timing he is faithful to keep every one of them. If hope seems lost, turn your eyes to the cross and find the one who gave everything for you. Your faith and hope are found only with him.

Holy God, I put my hope only in you. I trust that you keep all of your promises and that my hope will be fulfilled through your great love and faithfulness.

PASSIONS BECOME WEAPONS

Anyone who belongs to Christ has become a new person. The
old life is gone; a new life has begun!

2 CORINTHIANS 5:17 NLT

Some people fear that they will become unrecognizable when they
are newly created in Jesus Christ. Their old selves will be lost and all
the fun of life will be sucked into a giant black hole. This couldn't be
further from the truth!

Yes, the old has gone and the new has come. But we don't leave our
selves behind when we decide to follow Jesus, we just leave our sin!
Who we become in Christ is a beautiful blend of God-given gifts and
hearts submitted to obeying him. If you were a hilarious sinner before
knowing Christ, you can be an uproariously funny follower of Christ!
God has a plan for your hobbies and talents. When given over to God,
our passions become weapons in the hands of God to bring glory to
his kingdom.

You know me and my heart, God. Show me how my special
gifts and talents can be used for your kingdom. Show me, also,
any sinful behaviors that I should get rid of so that my life is a
beautiful and real testimony of what it looks like to faithfully
follow you.

JOY ALWAYS

Our hearts ache, but we always have joy. We are poor, but we give spiritual riches to others. We own nothing, and yet we have everything.

2 CORINTHIANS 6:10 NLT

It's easy to confuse joy with happiness; both bring to mind positive feelings, maybe even memories filled with laughter and smiles. But happiness is an emotion that comes and goes according to our circumstance; like sunshine on a cloudy day, it can be here one minute and gone the next.

The fullness of joy, however, is experienced in the heart. Regardless of one's surroundings or experience, the fullness of God's love pours forth a well-spring of unspeakable joy. As his beloved, you are given the gift of joy to keep you company no matter what trials life brings. You can *always have joy*.

Loving God, I pray that your joy would overflow in my life. Regardless of how happy I may feel, let joy pour out abundantly in my words and deeds so that those around me might know God's loving salvation.

LOVE DEFINITION

Love is patient and kind; love does not envy or boast; it is not arrogant or rude. It does not insist on its own way; it is not irritable or resentful; it does not rejoice at wrongdoing, but rejoices with the truth. Love bears all things, believes all things, hopes all things, endures all things.

1 CORINTHIANS 13:4-7 ESV

A good and right definition of love is central to understanding the message of God's Word. Without knowing how we are to love, we cannot fulfill the greatest commandment—to love God, or the second greatest commandment—to love our neighbors as ourselves. Unless we adopt God's way of loving one another, our efforts are in vain.

The Bible teaches that love is a commitment to live selflessly, generously, and humbly. It's not an emotion, but rather a decision to put other's needs above our own and to lay down our lives in service to them. This is how Jesus showed his love for us.

Jesus, you have shown me such abundant love and patience. Write your definition of love on my heart so that I can live it out in the world every day. Help me to put others first and love them the way you do!

NOTHING WRONG

Since we have been made right in God's sight by faith in his promises, we can have real peace with him because of what Jesus Christ our Lord has done for us.

ROMANS 5:1 TLB

What does complete peace look like? Perhaps it would mean a good night's sleep, free from anxious thoughts of tomorrow. Maybe it would mean gaining financial stability, or domestic harmony. Job security, family reconciliation, or depression might plague us, but peace brings the relief we've been praying for.

When we believe that God's promises for us are true, we can trust in the peace we gain through Jesus. When he is Lord of our hearts, we are no longer separated from God because of sin. We are brought into his family and counted as sons and daughters. One of the greatest benefits in this family is the great peace that rests on us. Nothing is wrong if we are right with God. Everything else will pass away, but his promise remains: we belong to him, and he never lets us go.

God, set my feet firmly on the peaceful promise I have through your Son, Jesus Christ. My worries and fears can be trusted to you, and peace will take their place.

ONE STEP AT A TIME

To him who is able to keep you from stumbling and to present you blameless before the presence of his glory with great joy, to the only God, our Savior, through Jesus Christ our Lord, be glory, majesty, dominion, and authority.

JUDE 24-25 ESV

This race called life is a long one; sometimes the road gets weary and our legs threaten to buckle underneath heavy burdens. How, then, do we persevere? When the cold rains of sorrow or the sharp winds of discouragement are at our backs, how do we press on and finish the race?

Hear this glorious news, beloved: God, whose majesty is matchless, is waiting to hold you up under the weight you are carrying. He lifts the burden to his own strong shoulders. He keeps you from slipping and falling away. What is greater, he brings you into his presence! Run your race today and hear the encouragement of your heavenly Father—his mighty shouts of everlasting joy—as you take it one holy step at a time. As long as you keep your eyes on him, you will finish victorious.

Lift me up, mighty God, when I stumble along this race of life. Whether the path is rugged or smooth, thank you for staying by my side, keeping me upright, and encouraging me with every step. I pray that I would hear your joyous voice today!

SACRIFICE OF PRAISE

Bring your petition. Come to the Lord and say, "O Lord, take away our sins; be gracious to us and receive us, and we will offer you the sacrifice of praise."

HOSEA 14:2 TLB

Songs of praise and worship are sometimes the last thing we feel like singing. A lamentation or a dirge feels more appropriate if we feel lonely, disappointed, or angry. How can we continue to praise our worthy God when we cannot find anything worthy of praise in our lives?

First, recognize the little things that are truly blessings: air in your lungs, God's love pouring over you, the salvation you have in Jesus Christ. Begin with these truths. And then, just as Hosea was instructed, offer God the *sacrifice of praise*. Sometimes praise comes at the cost of humbling ourselves and our situations to give God what he deserves. But God restores hearts a hundred-fold when they are submitted to him.

You alone, God, deserve my praise. You are always worthy. I am undeserving, yet you bless me. I am always falling, yet you lift me up. Thank you for your mercy and every good thing in my life. I praise your holy name!

HE CANNOT LIE

When God desired to show even more clearly to the heirs of the promise the unchangeable character of his purpose, he guaranteed it by an oath, so that through two unchangeable things, in which it is impossible that God would prove false, we who have taken refuge might be strongly encouraged to seize the hope set before us.

HEBREWS 6:17-18 NRSV

What a glorious hope we can have in our faithful and trustworthy God! He is the only true and honest Father, in whom we can find real safety. In a world filled with sin, it is easy for doubts, fears, and distrust to make their way into our hearts. We might become cynical and pessimistic, and then even the promises of our loving and dependable God can seem suspicious.

Instead, we can run to God for safety. Listen to the truth of his Word, where his promises have been fulfilled time and time again since creation. If Abraham trusted God to give him a son in his old age, we, too, can trust that God will fulfill his promises to us.

God, you are perfect and true. You alone are worthy of my trust and hope. Help me to see your promises and know that, unlike all of humanity, you cannot lie! Thank you for the truth of your promises.

A PERFECT PATH

All Scripture is inspired by God and is useful to teach us what is true and to make us realize what is wrong in our lives. It corrects us when we are wrong and teaches us to do what is right. God uses it to prepare and equip his people to do every good work.

2 TIMOTHY 3:16-17 NLT

God freely shares the secret to finding our life's great purpose, our reason for existence. For millennia, people have searched for this secret, some without ever finding a satisfactory answer. But God isn't trying to confuse us or delay the fulfillment of our purpose on earth. He wants us to understand it and pursue it with passion.

The Word of God contains every answer we will ever need. It is a divine tool meant to show us our right path. In it we find correction and rebuke but also encouragement and great wisdom. If we are humble enough to receive it, God's Word will equip us for our greatest purpose: serving one another for the kingdom of heaven.

Heavenly Father, you have a great plan for my life. Thank you for your perfect path. I ask for the humility to submit to your Word, obey your voice, and walk with endurance to fulfill my purpose.

SALVATION THROUGH HUMILITY

He gave himself for us so he might pay the price to free us from all evil and to make us pure people who belong only to him—people who are always wanting to do good deeds.
TITUS 2:14 NCV

Because of Adam and Eve's sin, we were all separated from God. God and sin cannot exist together. When Jesus Christ, who was fully God and fully man, shed his blood on the cross and died the death of a sinner, he made a way for sinners to be cleansed from their sin and exist in fellowship with God in the kingdom of heaven.

Salvation through Jesus' death is available to anyone who will humble themselves by confessing their own sin, repenting, and accepting that they are bought with the blood of Jesus. Salvation means you are free from all sin! This freedom sanctifies us. God works in us to make us more like Jesus, doing good for others and for the kingdom.

Jesus, thank you for your death on the cross and the salvation that is mine because of your suffering. Help me to serve you with gratitude and endurance, so others might find salvation in you.

THIRST SATISFIED

"If you only knew the gift God has for you and who you are speaking to, you would ask me, and I would give you living water .... Anyone who drinks this water will soon become thirsty again. But those who drink the water I give will never be thirsty again. It becomes a fresh, bubbling spring within them, giving them eternal life."

JOHN 4:10, 13-15 NLT

Jesus offers us something beyond earthly value, something impossible and holy and miraculous: a relationship with him. Only he truly knows us—our longings and passions and deepest desires—and only he can give us the satisfaction we are looking for.

Search the whole earth and you will never find anything that compares with the living water that Jesus offers. He loves you so much and waits patiently to satisfy you. Will you accept his gift today? Will you ask him to quench your thirst? He longs to satisfy your needs when you commit to a relationship with him.

Jesus, I want to drink from your living water. Pour your loving gifts over me, so my longing may finally be truly satisfied.

No Comparison

Moses stretched out his hand over the sea; and the Lord caused the sea to go back by a strong east wind all that night, and made the sea into dry land, and the waters were divided.

EXODUS 14:21 NKJV

God's mighty power is evident throughout the Bible. From creation, when he set the planets in motion and the stars in their place, to the shores of the Red Sea, where the Israelites were cornered by the Egyptian army, God's strength and miraculous power are unmatched. Who can compare to God? Who can do what he has done? Our God has no equal, in heaven or on earth.

The splendor of God's story is that the same mighty and matchless King who parted the seas and raised Lazarus from the dead offers us his strength every day. We, too, can fearlessly approach our enemies when the God of the universe directs our steps.

God of all creation, your works are mighty and glorious! You alone are worthy of all praise and honor. I am humbled to receive your strength and know that with it, I can overcome today's troubles.

RICH REWARDS

Do not throw away your confidence; it will be richly rewarded.
You need to persevere so that when you have done the will of
God, you will receive what he has promised.

HEBREWS 10:35-36 NIV

Remember the early days of your relationship with the Lord? Perhaps
you were a child, full of wonder and excitement. Maybe you were an
adult when you discovered his love, and it filled you to the brim with
joy. As you walk with Christ, life's ups and downs can get to you. The
confidence that you placed in him to save you from yourself may waver.

Don't lose heart! God promises to reward your faith. Place your trust
in him, and he will help you persevere through any situation. Breathe
in his peace today, and rejoice in it. When you feel like you may falter,
turn to him and seek the joy that only he can provide.

Lord, I pray I'd be restored to the excitement of the early
days of our relationship. Help me to remember your joy and
peace when I feel like I'm going to stumble. Thank you for the
promises you've made. I know you are faithful.

THE WAY TO VICTORY

Everyone who is a child of God conquers the world. And this is the victory that conquers the world—our faith. So the one who conquers the world is the person who believes that Jesus is the Son of God.

1 JOHN 5:4-5 NCV

Our greatest struggle this side of heaven is against the snares and deceptions of sin. Our faith in Jesus has set us free from the bonds of sin, but we are still susceptible to the lies of the enemy, who would love to see us wounded, tormented, and immobilized. When we are no longer effective for the kingdom of God, Satan is winning.

How, then, do we stay victorious? We must strengthen our weakness, attacking the sins in our lives and removing them piece by piece. This can be a painful process, but the more we battle sin, the more fully we experience the victorious life and all its blessings. Only by faith can we accomplish this.

Thank you, Jesus, for setting me free from the bondage of sin. I am no longer a slave, but have been set free! When the attacks of the enemy seem overwhelming, show me the way to victory.

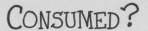

CONSUMED?

This I call to mind
and therefore I have hope:
Because of the LORD's great love we are not consumed,
for his compassions never fail.
LAMENTATIONS 3:21-22 NIV

What has consumed you today? Is it a deadline that you're worried about? A friend? A family member? Many of the things that weigh our hearts down are authentic burdens. Suffering in this life takes many different forms and we all encounter it one way or another. The author of Lamentations felt weighed down as well. And he knew the ticket to not being consumed with the worries of this world.

There are a few things we can take away from this prayer. First of all, we have to call to mind truth. It's not always the first thought that pops into our heads. In fact, worry and depression are often at the forefront of our minds. But this all changes when we remember the truth. And what is the truth that brings us strength? *God's great love.* Plain and simple. The steady, unchanging, strong love of God is what gives a heavy heart hope. Your burdens will always feel lighter in his presence.

Holy Spirit, please quicken me to call to mind your great love the next time I become consumed. I pray that as I have greater revelation of your love, I will have the grace to lay my burdens in your capable hands.

JOYFULLY I WAIT

I wait for the LORD, my whole being waits,
and in his word I put my hope.

PSALM 130:5 NIV

We so often think of waiting as hard, even unpleasant. But sometimes, waiting is wonderful: waiting to deliver great news, waiting for the birth of a child, the anticipation of giving a special gift.

When the thing we wait for is a good thing, waiting itself is a gift. This is how it is to wait for the Lord. With all our hope in him, the outcome is certain. The outcome is eternity. Let every part of us wait on him in joyful anticipation.

Lord, I love waiting for you! Because I know you bring only goodness, I can wait for you forever. Your Word is my hope, and it promises life and light forever with you. Gratefully, joyfully, I wait and I hope.

INSEPARABLE

I am convinced that neither death nor life, neither angels nor demons, neither the present nor the future, nor any powers, neither height nor depth, nor anything else in all creation will be able to separate us from the love of God that is in Christ Jesus our Lord.

ROMANS 8:38-39 NIV

Have you heard that before? Was it on the radio as you drove into work yesterday? Did you sing about it at church on Sunday? Was it part of your catechism as a child? *Nothing can separate you from God's love.* It seems as if we can hear something without it really taking root in our hearts. It's possible to hear the same thing so many times that you actually don't hear it at all anymore. Your heart becomes numb to the message.

Beloved, hear it again. And don't just hear it today but *soak* in its truth. Nothing can separate you from his love. Let that truth burn away your insecurities and your fears today. Let it stabilize your timid frame. Let it kick your anxieties to the curb. You will be ok. Why? Because there is no power strong enough to separate you from God's love. And this truth is enough to make your day great.

Father, while many other foundations can crack, thank you that nothing is strong enough to separate me from your love. Nothing in all of creation.

SETTING MY AFFECTION

Since you became alive again, so to speak, when Christ arose from the dead, now set your sights on the rich treasures and joys of heaven where he sits beside God in the place of honor and power. Let heaven fill your thoughts; don't spend your time worrying about things down here.

COLOSSIANS 3:1-2 TLB

There are many things that vie for our love and affection. We live in an incredibly materialistic culture. It's hard to be surrounded by that and not have it shape your desires. How can we not start wanting a million things we don't have when they are constantly being advertised before our very eyes?

One of the easiest ways to set your mind on things above is to really guard what comes into your mind in the first place. Sometimes you can't help the things that flash before your eyes, but many times you can. Purpose to set your heart on the things that are above.

Father, please help me turn from earthly affections and set my heart on things above—where you and your Son are seated.

INTELLIGENT LOVE

It is my prayer that your love may abound more and more, with knowledge and all discernment, so that you may approve what is excellent, and so be pure and blameless for the day of Christ.

PHILIPPIANS 1:9-10 ESV

As Christians, we are called to love others as Christ loved us. But does that mean we let our hearts go crazy, loving and accepting all? No! We are called to intelligent love. To love well. We should love what is good, what is right, what is pure. If we ask God for wisdom and knowledge when we put our hearts out there, he will give it to us and help us discern what is right and wrong.

The great thing about a relationship with Jesus is that it is a never-ending, constantly evolving, deepening kind of relationship. He will continue to help us grow and gain wisdom and understanding, so we can truly see what is excellent...and what is not.

Lord, thank you for your pure and blameless love. Help me to make wise choices with my heart today and every day as I live for you.

HE LIKES TO BE THANKED

Enter his gates with thanksgiving
and his courts with praise;
give thanks to him and praise his name.
PSALM 100:4 NIV

The morning alarms came too soon today. Whether they were in the form of children, an alarm clock, or a heavy heart that is restless even when its sleeping, your slumber is over. Your mind immediately starts going over your to-do list for the day as you stumble through your morning routine. You glance at your watch. How can you already be running late?

It is at this moment that you must stop to thank God. That's right, actually stop what you are doing, get down on your knees (to ensure you are stopping), and thank him. A thankful heart prepares the way for you to connect rightly with his heart. He isn't someone we use to get what we want. He is a sincere, loving provider for everything you will ever need. Pausing to thank him gives him the honor he's due. But it also kisses your heart with peace and joy in the midst of busy morning routines.

Loving Father, I enter into your presence now on another one of your creations—this day. Thank you for giving me another day on earth. Thank you for life in my body and your love. Help me walk in an attitude of thanksgiving unto you. I love you.

GOD SINGS!

He will take great delight in you;
in his love he will no longer rebuke you,
but will rejoice over you with singing.
ZEPHANIAH 3:17 NIV

The mastermind, creator, and executor of the design of the world is God. He is grand enough to create not just planets but an entire solar system, and not just one solar system, but many. He is infinitely larger than we can fathom. Yet, he pauses to sing. What does his face look like when he sings? Does the unapproachable light around him get brighter when song comes forth? What songs does he like? Is he partial to a certain style, or does he love them all? Is he a baritone or a bass? Or is he a certain mixture of them both that we can't conceive of?

We can only inquire of the answers to those questions. But there is one thing Scripture tells us about his singing: the *object* of his song. It is you. That's right, out of the myriad of options he could sing about, he chose you. He sings *about* you and *over* you. When it's quiet, when you're alone, when it's chaotic, he sings with words that are fueled by his untamed loved for you.

Father, help me hear your song today. When I am stressed, alone, worried or afraid, help me hear the song of deliverance that you sing over me. Thank you for your strong love.

THE ONE YOU WORSHIP

Who has measured the waters in the hollow of his hand
and marked off the heavens with a span,
enclosed the dust of the earth in a measure
and weighed the mountains in scales
and the hills in a balance?
To whom then will you compare me,
that I should be like him? says the Holy One.
Lift up your eyes on high and see:
who created these?
He who brings out their host by number,
calling them all by name,
by the greatness of his might,
and because he is strong in power
not one is missing.

ISAIAH 40:12, 25-26 ESV

Here you are spending time with Jesus today. You have carved out this moment, paused your day, to commune with your Maker. Perhaps you have come with a list of things to discuss with him. Perhaps you are simply hungry to hear his voice.

Today, let him tell you who he is. It will invoke worship, security, and trust.

Holy One, I can hardly believe that you created all that and yet invite me to call you Father. I see the stars, sun, and moon on a daily basis. Help me never to lose the wonder in your creation as it points to an almighty, powerful Creator. I worship you today.

JUNE

The LORD God is a sun and shield;

the LORD bestows favor and honor;

no good thing does he withhold

from those whose walk is blameless.

PSALM 84:11 NIV

WISER THAN YOU

With whom did He take counsel, and who instructed Him,
And taught Him in the path of justice?
Who taught Him knowledge,
And showed Him the way of understanding?
ISAIAH 40:14 NKJV

Do you find yourself questioning God's movement on the earth? As an excellent Father, we know he only has our best interests in mind. Yet, when we see sin running rampant and lives devastated by it, sometimes we wonder what he is doing. We question if he really sees. He does. He sees it all. Every ounce of pain and suffering is not lost on him, and his heart is not cold toward it.

Jesus is coming back and he will come with pure justice and power. Everyone will give an account of their actions. He is a perfect judge and he will rule well. He is altogether just and compassionate. He is indeed coming back and he will make all the wrong things right.

Father, thank you that you are a righteous judge; it is simply who you are. When I don't see you, I will choose to trust you are who you say you are.

PRECIOUS, HONORED, LOVED

Because you are precious in my eyes,
and honored, and I love you,
I give men in return for you,
peoples in exchange for your life.

ISAIAH 43:4 ESV

Have you ever read a love letter that wasn't intended for you? If written well, it offers a picture into someone's heart that is wide open with love. Unguarded, unprotected, laying their heart on the line because of their love for someone else. You almost feel embarrassed reading something so intimate.

Do you hear the sweet, tender word of God written for you today? You have been called precious and honored. You are treasured and protected. God will never take advantage of you. His love for you is pure.

Father, I receive the words you have given me today. You love me. Help me not to reject your love, but to grow because of it.

LIFT MY HEAVY HEART

If you pour yourself out for the hungry
and satisfy the desire of the afflicted,
then shall your light rise in the darkness
and your gloom be as the noonday.
ISAIAH 58:10 ESV

In God's kingdom, he does things differently. Things that are
discarded or pushed aside here on earth are valued by God. Weak,
disenfranchised, afflicted people catch God's eye much quicker than
they catch ours. God sees their affliction and he chooses to meet
their needs through his body. Unfortunately, sometimes we are too
consumed with our own trials to notice the suffering around us.

If we pour ourselves out for others in need, our light will rise and our
darkness will lessen. As we meet other people's needs, God meets our
needs and lifts our heaviness.

Thank you, God, that you care about my heart even when
there are others who hurt more. Help me to serve them so I am
not so focused on myself. Help me to see those around me and
truly care for them.

NOT HOME YET

"There are many rooms in my Father's house; I would not tell you this if it were not true. I am going there to prepare a place for you."

JOHN 14:2 NCV

Our homes on earth are significant in our lives. They are where we lay our heads, where we display our style, and where we commune with family and friends. But, truth be told, they are imperfect. Try as you might, you can never get that paint color right on your wall. Or when you buy the bedding that you love, you notice it has begun to fray. None of it lasts forever.

That is part of the reason that Jesus told us about our eternal homes. He wants us to look forward to them. He is preparing a place for us. Places that were designed for us to enjoy. We don't know exactly what they will be like, but we do know that the one who is preparing them is the same one who knows our tastes better than anyone else.

Jesus, thank you that you are preparing a place for me. Thank you that my greatest joy in heaven won't be the place you prepared for me, but it will be dwelling your very presence.

IMAGE BEARER

God created man in His own image, in the image of God He created him; male and female He created them.

GENESIS 1:27 NASB

Western culture has done us no favors in having healthy body images. The women we see on magazines have doctored-up images, the rich and famous often aren't healthy, and every ad targeted at us tells us to hide our age. Be reminded that today you are more than what you look like. Your value is much deeper than your appearance.

The King of all creation has placed tremendous value on your life. When he was masterfully designing all of creation, in the first five days, nothing bore his image. It was his handiwork but not his actual *image*. Sharing God's image was reserved exclusively for one part of creation—man and woman.

Father, forgive me for believing the lies that say my value is in how I look. Thank you that I have beauty, value, and worth simply because I was made in your image.

FACIAL EXPRESSIONS

Answer me, O Lord, for your steadfast love is good;
according to your abundant mercy, turn to me.
PSALM 69:16 NRSV

What do you think God's face looks like when you engage him
in conversation? If you view him as irritable or moody, you will
approach him with timidity and fear. If think he is unpredictable,
you will walk on eggshells, unsure of how he will respond. It's true;
God is not static in his emotions. He expresses himself freely in
Scripture. Circumstances invoke anger, joy, and compassion in him.
But his emotions, unlike ours, are not fickle. They are reasonable and
justifiable.

What's important for you to know is that God's heart toward you is
like that of a compassionate father. If you have chosen to love him,
you are his child. He loves you and his heart is inclined toward you.
He desires for you to approach him, and he smiles as you do. He is
eager to hear from you today.

Father, thank you that you invite me to boldly come to you
when I need you. Thank you that the invitation isn't to come in
fear. You eagerly await my steps toward you and welcome me
with a hug.

Inward Renewal

We do not lose heart. Though outwardly we are wasting away,
yet inwardly we are being renewed day by day.

2 CORINTHIANS 4:16 NIV

Sometimes when you wake up, you don't feel rested at all. Your back
might ache, there could be bags under your eyes, and your skin may
seem a little (or a lot) looser. You know you don't look or feel like you
did when you were younger, but you can't quite remember exactly
when you started aging. You think, "Wasn't my mother older than me
when she looked like this?"

Today, own your aging instead of wishing it away. Everyone is
growing older. It's nothing to be ashamed of. In many cultures, people
aspire to be older because it means they are wiser and more widely
respected. More importantly, getting older in the Lord also means that
you are being renewed day by day. Your aim when you wake should
not be how you can alter your appearance to make yourself look
younger; rather, it should be how you can be renewed in your heart,
mind, and soul.

Father, help me see that inward renewal is far more valuable—
and eternal—than outward renewal.

DELAYED OBEDIENCE

"Blessed rather are those who hear the word of God and keep it!"
LUKE 11:28 ESV

There are people who seem to have a closer walk with God than others. While there are many contributing factors, one of the chief reasons is obedience. Put simply, when God asks something of them, they obey. It might seem like an issue isn't urgent or critical to us, so we make excuses: "Maybe someone else can give money to the missionaries," or, "the lie was only small," or, "let another person bring her a meal; I have too much on my plate."

Excuses, or even delayed obedience, can actually be disobedience. When we disobey his promptings, we have no idea of the chain effect. We should know that when God puts something on our hearts to do, he has chosen the exact time for it.

Father, help me to listen for your prompting and to be quick to obey. I want to be pleasing to you, choosing to lay down my own plans and pick up yours.

BETRAYED WITH A KISS

Judas came, one of the twelve, and with him a crowd with swords and clubs, from the chief priests and the scribes and the elders. Now the betrayer had given them a sign, saying, "The one I will kiss is the man. Seize him and lead him away under guard." And when he came, he went up to him at once and said, "Rabbi!" And he kissed him.

MARK 14:43-45 ESV

Has anyone ever professed agreement, loyalty, or love, but you knew their heart was far from you? Sometimes it's the look in their eyes that gives them away. Sometimes you really believed you were in sincere agreement until their actions didn't follow through. Betrayal can be crushing.

We can do this at times with God. It's easy to slip into church, boldly singing worship songs, without dealing with the state of our hearts. We appear to be kissing him with our love and adoration, yet we are firmly holding part of our hearts back. God is not shocked by this—just as Jesus wasn't shocked by Judas' betrayal. He knew it would happen even as he washed Judas' feet! If you are holding back from God, know that he would wash your feet today in the hope of winning your heart.

Father, help me give all of my heart to you today. I don't want to betray you with insincere kisses. I want to remain loyal to you, loving you with all that I am.

LITTLE OFFERINGS

A cheerful look brings joy to the heart;
good news makes for good health.
PROVERBS 15:30 NLT

Don't dismiss the value of little things. More often than we realize,
the Holy Spirit prompts us throughout each day to do things that
bring glory to the Father. These little promptings can come in the
form of thoughts, which makes them easy to dismiss. Instead, make
today a day of little offerings to the one who made you. Offer a smile
to someone who hasn't "earned" it. Say a prayer for the worker who
was sharp. Meet that need you overheard someone talking about.
These things may seem small to you at the time, but you have no idea
the implications of your obedience.

There is a reason the Holy Spirit highlights people around you; it's no
coincidence that they are there. Your smile might be the first one they
have gotten in a long time. Conversely, a stern or unnecessary cold
word has the power to ruin their moment or even their day. Choose
to give them a look of love that will bring joy to their heart.

Father, help me be faithful with my little offerings to others
and you. Help my smile lighten the load for others.

SIMPLY GENTLE

The tongue has the power of life and death,
and those who love it will eat its fruit.

PROVERBS 18:21 NIV

We have all been given a profoundly powerful tool—our tongues. As children of God, we have a unique ability to speak life with our words; therefore, we should choose them carefully. Once spoken, words cannot be taken back. Quick, harsh words can take a conversation that was otherwise amiable and turn it into a firestorm.

Today, ask God to purify your language. Ask him for the grace to give gentle answers. Test him in this. You will see that as you speak gently with others, peace will come into conversations that would have otherwise been tense.

Jesus, please train me to use my tongue well. Help me use it for your glory. Show me how I can honor you more with it.

WHERE DO YOU WALK?

How blessed is the man who does not walk
in the counsel of the wicked,
Nor stand in the path of sinners,
Nor sit in the seat of scoffers!
But his delight is in the law of the LORD,
And in His law he meditates day and night.
    PSALM 1:1-2 NASB

We can be followers of Jesus but be surrounded by all the wrong things. Eventually, if we have surrounded ourselves with poor influences, we become conformed to their image—not the other way around. Therefore, it's important to take stock of your surroundings.

Who do you walk with? What counsel do you allow into your life? Who are you standing with? Do your friends delight in sinning? Where are you sitting? Do the people you are seated with scoff at God? There are times we will associate with the world because we want to win them to the Lord. But they shouldn't be our closest friends. Instead, our delight should come from God's teaching; it is our true joy and strength.

God, help me walk, stand, and sit in your presence so I can delight in all you are. Keep me rooted in the counsel of your Word. Only there will I be given the very best advice.

HIDING HIS WORD

I have stored up your word in my heart,
that I might not sin against you.
PSALM 119:11 ESV

There is tremendous value in taking time to memorize the Word of God. It's one thing to breeze through it in the morning but an entirely different thing to chew on and digest its teaching. When you really digest God's Word, it goes from your head into your heart.

One of the best ways to store his Word in your heart is to memorize portions of Scripture. When you memorize something, you repeat it in your head. This simple act naturally causes you to think about the Word of God more than other idle or anxious thoughts. Furthermore, the nature of *storing* means you are obtaining something now that you will need at a later date. It means you see the importance of keeping it to benefit you in the future.

Father, please give me the wisdom and grace to store your Word in my heart now so it will be there in my hour of need.

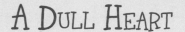

A DULL HEART

Turn my eyes from looking at worthless things;
and give me life in your ways.

PSALM 119:37 ESV

Do you find your love for God growing cold? An intimate walk with God requires time. Any relationship does. A relationship where one party invests very little will become strained. Mistrust can develop where there is no cause, simply because the two aren't spending time together.

Take inventory; what in your heart is causing a dull or bored attitude toward God? Sometimes the cause is that you are investing time in other pursuits and you don't have time for your walk with him. Are there "worthless things" that have captivated your heart? Pray and ask God to give you his strength that will enable you to turn your eyes from them. He will readily help a humbled heart, igniting it with life.

Father, give me more of your Spirit that I might turn away from everything that hinders my walk with you. Thank you that you're my biggest cheerleader and that you are for me as I seek you.

MEDITATION

Make me understand the way of Your precepts;
So shall I meditate on Your wonderful works.
PSALM 119:27 NKJV

Meditation can get a bad rap. Other religions encourage meditation to bring about holiness. They encourage followers to find some created entity that gives them life and mull it over and over in their head until it brings about change. What use is there is meditating on something created when you can meditate on the *Creator*? Scripture actually encourages meditation all throughout the Psalms. There is tremendous value in giving enormous amounts of time and mental energy to God and his works.

God reveals his heart in the ways in which he moves on the earth. Take time to meditate on his works. Remember how he parted the Red Sea, poured his Spirit on men in a locked room, and walked on water. Let them not be mere stories but miraculous works of an affectionate God.

Father, as I meditate on how you moved in the past, reveal your character and heart toward me.

OPEN MY EYES

Open my eyes, that I may behold
wondrous things out of your law.

PSALM 119:18 ESV

Has your Bible reading become laborious? It's not unusual for your time in the Word to become difficult, or even boring, during various seasons. When you go through a time like this, it's important to remember a couple of things. First of all, while God's Word might be difficult for you to digest, he is not. There is nothing boring or dull about the God of the universe. Recognize that your struggle is with the discipline of studying the Word—not with him.

Secondly, pray and ask the Spirit to help you. The Holy Spirit's job is to point you to the Father, so he delights in revealing God to you through the written Word. You need the Spirit to do that which you can't. Just ask.

Holy Spirit, I ask that you would open my eyes and show me the wondrous things that are in your law. Reveal to me who you are through the written Word.

MY COUNSELORS

Your testimonies are my delight;
they are my counselors.
PSALM 119:24 ESV

Many of us go through a season where we need a counselor.
Sometimes the trauma and drama of life require another voice to
give us direction through the wilderness we find ourselves in. A
good counselor who continually points someone to Jesus is worth
their weight in gold. But we should be quick to seek God first before
immediately running to others.

Through God's Word, the testimonies that we read have the power
to give us counsel when needed. They give us direction, comfort,
wisdom, and hope. When you read Biblical testimonies, you see that
God has never left his people and that there is always reason to hope.

Father, thank you for the testimonies in your Word. Reveal
them to me today that I might receive the hope and wisdom I
need right now.

HE REMEMBERS

Though a thousand generations pass he never forgets his
promise, his covenant with Abraham and Isaac.
PSALM 105:8-9 TLB

God is a covenant keeper. He has made promises with specific people
since the very beginning of time. That, in and of itself, does not make
him unique. People make promises and vows all the time. The critical
difference between our promises and God's promises is that he never,
ever forgets or breaks his. Unfortunately, because there is so much
mistrust in many of our hearts, it's hard for us to believe that.

Beloved, you have a God that will never forget a promise he's made.
If he makes it, you can count on him fulfilling it. His track record on
this is perfect. We have watched him be faithful to every promise he's
ever made through the course of history. What's more, he remembers
these covenants through every generation. Be careful not to apply
attributes to him that are human. He is much better than we are.

Father, thank you that you remember every covenantal
promise you have ever made, and you have never broken one.
Your faithfulness never ceases!

It's Okay to Be Weak

For the sake of Christ, then, I am content with weaknesses, insults, hardships, persecutions, and calamities. For when I am weak, then I am strong.

2 CORINTHIANS 12:10 ESV

In our relationship with God, both parties aren't intended to be strong. In his perfect design, the relationship works because we, the created are finite and weak. We are often deceived into thinking that God wants us to be strong like he is. In his kingdom, though, true strength is marked by those embracing their weakness and calling out to the one who is stronger, in a true display of humility.

You might feel like you need to project strength in order to be treated with respect, but this isn't the way it works with God. He isn't asking you to prove yourself to him. He is asking you to embrace your humanity. That humble act is actually what makes you strong because it gives God permission to fill you with his strength.

Father, help me to turn to you in my weakness and not pretend to be strong. Please fill me with your strength to do that which lies before me today.

It Is Finished

When Jesus had received the sour wine, He said, "It is finished!"
And bowing His head, He gave up His spirit.

JOHN 19:30 NKJV

When Jesus was dying on the cross, he spoke a few things to those gathered around. It is a worthwhile study to spend some time chewing on what he said. He knew he had mere hours, if not minutes, left on earth. He knew what his mother needed to hear from him as she watched him suffer a slow death. He knew his best friend needed a game plan on how to care for his mother. He knew the thief needed to understand that it wasn't too late. And he knew what we would need to know today, over two thousand years later.

There is a phrase that Jesus uttered that should give us cause for deep, internal rest here on earth and in heaven: "It is finished." It is still finished today. His work was complete. He permanently defeated death so that anyone who wishes to can enter into eternal life.

Thank you Lord that your finished work on the cross over two thousand years ago can bring me inner rest today.

FUELED BY LOVE

I know your works, your toil and your patient endurance,
and how you cannot bear with those who are evil, but have
tested those who call themselves apostles and are not, and
found them to be false. I know you are enduring patiently and
bearing up for my name's sake, and you have not grown weary.
REVELATION 2:2-3 ESV

In the book of Revelation, in chapters two and three, there are seven
letters written to seven separate churches in Asia Minor (modern day
Turkey). These letters were written by Jesus, through John, to real
churches with real believers. Many of the letters contain both words
of affirmation and correction. The church in Ephesus gets praised for
many things: patient endurance, hating evil, and not growing weary
amidst hardships. This sounds wonderful until you get to Jesus' word
of correction: they have abandoned their first love.

If we weren't humans ourselves, it would be hard to believe this could
happen. How could those believers accomplish so much "for God," yet
have ceased to love him like they first did? Beloved, we are all capable
of doing things for God that are not first fueled by love for him.
Perhaps for a season we need to cease our activities and just spend
time loving God the way we used to.

Jesus, help me place you as my first love before I do things to
impress you. I know you desire my heart more than anything
else, and I want you to have it.

FEAR NOT

There is no fear in love; but perfect love casts out fear, because
fear involves punishment, and the one who fears is not
perfected in love.

1 JOHN 4:18 NASB

Fear not. Many people, products, and philosophies tell us not to be
afraid. Some will say our fears aren't founded. Some just try to help
us mitigate our fears. But the truth is that only Jesus can tell us not
to be afraid because he is the only one with the power to annihilate
your fears. He is the only one who has perfect love.

Because Jesus conquered fear and death on the cross, you can have
peace today. Fear not because Jesus is your advocate in heaven. Fear not
because his love is perfect. Fear not because he told you not to be afraid.

Jesus, give me the grace to obey you and choose not to fear.
Thank you that your love conquers all my fears.

THE STORY ISN'T FINISHED

When I saw him, I fell at his feet as though dead. But he laid his right hand on me, saying, "Fear not, I am the first and the last, and the living one. I died, and behold I am alive forevermore, and I have the keys of Death and Hades."
REVELATION 1:17-18 ESV

John the apostle was given a priceless gift as he sat in exile on the island of Patmos. He was given a revelation of Jesus Christ that was intended to show the things that would soon take place. Throughout the book of Revelation, Jesus makes it clear that the story isn't over.

While we might see sin and injustice abound, we don't need to fear. When all else is shaking around us, we aren't afraid. Satan does not have the final say. Jesus is the last one who will speak and the one who will have victory. Your advocate and victorious king is coming!

Jesus, thank you that you are returning and that you have the final say. Help me wait for that day without fear.

LABELS

There is neither Jew nor Gentile, neither slave nor free, nor is there male and female, for you are all one in Christ Jesus.
GALATIANS 3:28 NIV

Growing up we have a tendency to label people based on their strengths and weaknesses. This person is an athlete or that person is a musician. Some of these labels are intended to compliment, but many can be damaging. As we assign labels to people, they begin to define themselves by those labels—for better or worse.

It's liberating when we take the labels off and just *be*. The labels listed in the passage above were prominently divisive at the time. They mattered too much. Paul reminds us that we are all one in Christ Jesus. Let's remove labels from ourselves, stop putting them on others, and just be who we were created to be.

Jesus, help me view myself and others with the most important label: your children. I release others that I have limited by the label I placed on them, and I ask you to help me shake off the labels put on me by others.

QUICK FIX

Let's not get tired of doing what is good. At just the right time
we will reap a harvest of blessing if we don't give up.
GALATIANS 6:9 NLT

In our culture, quick fixes for problems are sought after and
esteemed. No one wants a slow, gradual weight loss plan. If there is
a way to drop pounds in a weekend, we are willing to pay a pretty
penny to make it happen. Many are deceived into thinking that their
best way out of debt is to wishfully throw money into a lottery in
hopes that they can get all the cash they need to be debt free.

In reality, almost everything that is of any real worth takes time. It
takes time to build relationships. It takes time to become good at a
hobby or sport. And it takes time to build new eating habits that will
allow you to lose weight long term. Quick fixes don't really fix the
deeper issues. Let's stick with God's long-term plan instead.

Father, give me the wisdom I need to not be swayed by all the
quick fixes that come my way. Help me to remain faithful in my
habits. I thank you in advance for the harvest I will reap.

HELP ME REMEMBER

Let my soul be at rest again,
for the LORD has been good to me.
PSALM 116:7 NLT

This psalm gives a great picture of the mind telling the soul to calm down. Sometimes we have to talk to ourselves in order to really believe the truth. The psalmist knew that the Lord had been faithful to him in the past. He knows his soul has experienced internal rest before and he believes he can experience it again.

This isn't just hopeful self-talk. The Lord's goodness really does bring rest. And God's goodness can be experienced every day. We just need to take the time to remember it.

Holy Spirit, please remind me of all the times you have been good to me in the past. I believe that you will be good to me again because you are good.

YOU CAN'T CONTROL THE RAIN

He covers the heavens with clouds,
prepares rain for the earth,
makes grass grow on the hills...
The Lord takes pleasure in those who fear him,
in those who hope in his steadfast love.

PSALM 147:8, 11 NRSV

How is the weather where you are? Have you had endless sunny days with not a dark cloud to be seen? Has the temperature been perfect? Not too cold, not too hot? Or has it been steadily raining? Perhaps it's not even really *rain*; maybe it's more of a constant drizzle that leaves everything damp. Sometimes it's those drizzles that bring weariness— they just don't seem to let up.

As God would have it, you can't control the rain. Life's circumstances are such that many are simply out of our control. And sometimes when one thing goes wrong, it seems to be an invitation for countless others. One fact that you should lean on is that many circumstances are out of our control. Because you can't control them, don't exhaust yourself trying. Instead, give yourself to the one thing you can control: your response to the rain. Ask God to give you vision and hope that is not dictated by the weather. That allows you to see above the clouds and gives you the perspective you need.

Holy Spirit, you say that when I pass through the waters, you will be with me, and the rivers won't overwhelm me. I believe you. Give me your perspective today.

LIMITATIONS

He knows our frame;
he remembers that we are dust.
PSALM 103:14 ESV

Does your body not do what you want it to do? As we age, we notice that we aren't able to do the things we used to be able to do. Sometimes it isn't age that causes this; sometimes our bodies just simply breakdown. Our minds don't seem as sharp after a long day. Or the demands around us from the people that we love the most seem impossible to meet.

God made you human; therefore, you have definite limitations in your abilities. He does not. God never asked you to be like him. He is the one who designed your frame, and he is intimately acquainted with human frailty. If you have expectations on yourself that are different than that, you need to adjust them.

Father, thank you that you remember that I am dust. You are not disappointed with my weak frame. You designed it that way so I could cling to your infinite strength.

REWARD OF PERSEVERANCE

The soul of the sluggard craves and gets nothing,
while the soul of the diligent is richly supplied.
PROVERBS 13:14 ESV

Working hard is one of the most rewarding experiences God gives us. There is something extremely satisfying about putting in a good day's work. When you set your hand to a task and choose not to quit until it's complete, the sense of accomplishment is great. It can't be bought.

Perseverance isn't just handed to us on a silver platter, though. It is earned—primarily through a task that comes with a strong temptation to quit. Remember that the Lord will reward your diligence and perseverance over laziness. In your perseverance God will richly supply your soul.

Father, give me endurance where I lack it. I cannot do this on my own. I ask for your strength to fill me where I am weak so that I might persevere.

DON'T QUIT

We can rejoice, too, when we run into problems and trials, for
we know that they are good for us—they help us learn to be
patient. And patience develops strength of character in us and
helps us trust God more each time we use it until finally our
hope and faith are strong and steady

ROMANS 5:3-4 TLB

That's one of the best pieces of advice you can give to someone
enduring a trial. Just encourage them not to give up. Trials come in
many different shapes and sizes, but one thing is true of them all—they
wear you down. If that weren't true, then it wouldn't really be a trial.

Trial, by mere definition of the word, indicates that what we're going
through is pushing us past the limits that we have. Trials are a strain
on us emotionally, physically, and sometimes spiritually. But they aren't
foreign to the body of Christ. You aren't alone in your trial. Persevere
that you might know the hope he awards those who don't quit.

Father, I ask for new endurance and perseverance today. Thank
you that this trial isn't lost on you. You will use it for your
glory and my growth.

JULY

Praise the Lord, because he is good;
sing praises to him, because it is pleasant.

PSALM 135:3 NCV

PAST, PRESENT, OR FUTURE?

Hear, O Israel: The LORD is our God, the LORD alone. You shall love the LORD your God with all your heart, and with all your soul, and with all your might.

DEUTERONOMY 6:4-5 NRSV

Where are you living today? Better yet, where is your heart focused? Sometimes occurrences of the past are constantly cycling through our minds. We replay them like a movie. At times these are happy memories and at others they are memories full of sadness and regret. Either way, they both remain in our past.

We can respond the same way to our future. We often worry about what is to come and whether or not we are prepared. Or we look forward to the days that lie ahead, wishfully assuming they will be better than today. And herein lies the problem; staying in the past or constantly looking to the future means that you miss *today*. And today is all you are promised. So, seek his kingdom and enjoy his provision for today.

Father, help me not stare back at my past or always look to my future but steadfastly serve you and know you today.

A Full Life

Not neglecting to meet together, as is the habit of some, but encouraging one another, and all the more as you see the Day drawing near.

HEBREWS 10:25 ESV

Most people's worlds are full. Everyone has twenty-four hours in a day. No one has more; no one has less. And we all fill those hours with something. As a believer, it is crucial to spend a good portion of your time with other Christians. Christianity is fully expressed when believers are together. As a body we are supposed to teach, encourage, and love one another.

Not neglecting meeting together has a two-fold purpose. The first is that you give courage to others where theirs might be lost. The second? You help them persevere as the Day of the Lord comes closer. But it's not just a one-way street—meeting with other believers offers you the same benefits. Why wouldn't you want that?

Father, remind me that I am not supposed to do this faith thing on my own. Remind me to meet with my brothers and sisters so I can encourage them and be encouraged myself.

A Guarded Mind

The peace of God, which transcends all understanding, will guard your hearts and your minds in Christ Jesus.

PHILIPPIANS 4:7 NIV

Perhaps a guarded mind should be one of the first disciplines we exercise when we come to Christ. Our thought life is such an integral part of who we are and all our actions flow from it. Prior to salvation, most people will let their thoughts roll without restraint or consideration. After we are saved, however, we have the Holy Spirit, and he is quick to bring awareness where there once was none.

You might notice that some of your thoughts are ungodly, but because you aren't acting on them, you dismiss them. However, the Holy Spirit wants to bring even your thought life under submission to God. This is truly for your own benefit. God's peace is intended to guard both your heart and your mind. Receive his peace as a guard over both.

Holy Spirit, please teach me how to submit not just my actions but my thought life to you. I need you to give me the strength to break old thought patterns.

PROMISE OF FREEDOM

Jesus said to the Jews who had believed him, "If you abide in my word, you are truly my disciples, and you will know the truth, and the truth will set you free."

JOHN 8:31-32 ESV

We are incredibly blessed to live in a free country where we can express our ideas and beliefs, worship openly, and live our lives as we see fit. Our Constitution was written to ensure freedom for all citizens—national, individual, and political. There is one freedom, however, that no constitution, regardless of how comprehensive, can promise, and that is spiritual freedom. Liberation of the soul only comes through forgiveness offered to us through Christ. When our sins are forgiven and we stay faithful to the truth, then we are truly free.

Maybe it's time for a "freedom check" this morning. Is your life truly a reflection of the Christ in whom you say you believe? Are you faithfully in the Word and obedient to it? If not, perhaps it's time to get back on track. Then you can be confident that no matter what you face, the God of truth will guide you to freedom.

Lord, I want to be faithful to your Word. Forgive me when I neglect it. I want to truly be your disciple and to fill my mind with truth that will set me free.

LIFELONG SLAVERY

Since therefore the children share in flesh and blood, he himself likewise partook of the same things, that through death he might destroy the one who has the power of death, that is, the devil, and deliver all those who through fear of death were subject to lifelong slavery.

HEBREWS 2:14-15 ESV

The fear of death can rob someone of truly living. Culturally speaking, this fear has permeated the marketplace. There are thousands of products that seek to resist the aging process and help us eek out another few years of life. From pills, to supplements, to meditation, many promote themselves as helping you avoid death for just a little bit longer.

While we shouldn't seek to end our lives, as believers we shouldn't be afraid of death either. For us, death has lost its sting because we know that it is simply a means to eternal life. When you're afraid of something, you can become a slave to it. Let Jesus deliver you from fear so you can truly start living!

Jesus, thank you that you have the power to deliver me from my fear of death. I ask now that you would do just that. I trust that even in death you will be with me.

INSEPARABLE

We know how much God loves us, and we have put our trust in his love. God is love, and all who live in love live in God, and God lives in them.

1 JOHN 4:16 NLT

God's love for you is the most powerful force in the entire universe. This is not a trite little phrase. It is an unchanging truth about God. He is all that love is. His very nature is that of love. His love is much stronger, consistent, and fearless than ours. And nothing has the power to stop it. If something could have stopped God's love, it would have succeeded right before Jesus' death on the cross.

Even the impending death of his Son did not stop God's love. In fact, it's where he demonstrated it best. Think about God's incredible love for you today. Allow the reality of it to sink in deep. You cannot be separated from his powerful love.

Father, thank you that your love for me is stronger than my love for you. Help me be strengthened today by your strong, unfailing love for me.

STEADY LOVE

The LORD is merciful and gracious,
slow to anger and abounding in steadfast love.
PSALM 103:8 ESV

God loves you with a steadfast love today. In fact, he has loved you with a steadfast love every day of your life and will continue to into eternity. God's love is firmly fixed. It is absolutely and unequivocally unwavering. This isn't just something we can infer. It is a truth that has been tested and proven throughout all time. As he loved in the beginning, so we see him loving now.

Not only does God have steady love toward you today, he *abounds* in it. He has an overflowing, ridiculous amount of love for you—enough that it can fill you up and spill out to others around you.

Father, thank you for your steadfast love. Help me receive your stabilizing love today and point others toward it as well.

Rules, Rules, Rules

The kingdom of God is not eating and drinking, but righteousness and peace and joy in the Holy Spirit.

ROMANS 14:17 NKJV

For some who have grown up in the church, all they can think of when they think about God are rules. At times we have done a poor job of representing God when we speak of him. It is easy to talk about everything we should and shouldn't do as Christians. The problem with doing this is that we often forget to talk about Christ himself.

Jesus did not come to lay down a bunch of rules for us to live by. He came to invite us into a relationship with his Father through his blood. Good relationships are so much more than two people obeying rules. God doesn't want you to simply obey him. He wants you to know his life, joy, and peace as you become his friend.

Father, thank you that your kingdom is about so much more than rules. Please help me know your love that gives me the strength to obey you, so I might walk in righteousness, peace, and joy.

ROOTED AND ESTABLISHED

That Christ may dwell in your hearts through faith, as you are being rooted and grounded in love.
EPHESIANS 3:17 NRSV

As a plant grows, we rarely take the time to see what is growing below the surface. At a quick glance, we only admire all that we see on top of the soil: a flourishing, healthy plant. However, no plant looks like that without some strong, sturdy roots in the soil. Those roots are what allow that plant to flourish and be beautiful.

For us to thrive as we are intended, our roots need to be firmly established in love. And not just any love. In God's strong, unfailing love. For us to be all that God has called us to be, we must be 100% confident of his unfailing love. His love is stable and secure, and he intends for us to plunge the very roots of our heart deep into it. It will sustain you, calm you, and cause you to thrive.

Father, give me the grace to trust your love for me. Help me establish my roots in your love and nothing else.

MUCH BETTER

Let me hear of your unfailing love each morning,
for I am trusting you.
Show me where to walk,
for I give myself to you.

PSALM 143:8 NLT

We all see God through our human lenses because we are finite. When we hear of his attributes, we often put a human spin on them—many times subconsciously. If we hear that he is love, we think that means he loves like we do. If we hear that he is patient, we think of the most patient person we know. And if we hear that he is kind, we picture a human that exhibits kindness. But in the back of all our human examples lie failure. Because at some point even the most loving, patient, and kind person you know will fail.

You see, we are silently accusing God in our disbelief. We question the one who has never lied. We suggest he's incapable of the perfect love that he has professed. A sick feeling stirs in our gut. *At some point, this perfect love, patience, and kindness will run out.* He is much better than we think. His attributes are unmarred and untainted. He cannot fail.

Father, thank you that you are who you say you are. Help me in my unbelief.

I Sinned. Now What?

You younger men, likewise, be subject to your elders; and all of you, clothe yourselves with humility toward one another, for God is opposed to the proud, but gives grace to the humble.
1 PETER 5:5 NASB

We have all been there. We did the thing we were never planning on doing. Sometimes we shock even ourselves. It's a human problem—one we will wrestle with until the day we die. God doesn't expect perfection from us. In fact, he made a way for us explicitly because we are not perfect. We need a Savior.

All God asks for is our humility: humility that comes to him and confesses the sin that we have walked in. God won't deal with us according to our sin because Jesus already paid the price. We can receive his forgiveness without trembling in fear of what he will do to us. His forgiveness is already available and waiting for us today.

Father, I know that you oppose the proud but give grace to the humble. Help me to humbly come to your arms of grace after I have sinned.

GET A GLIMPSE

A day in your courts is better
than a thousand elsewhere.
I would rather be a doorkeeper in the house of my God
than dwell in the tents of wickedness.
PSALM 84:10 ESV

God rewards his children with wonderful gifts. He loves to honor anyone that takes the time to seek him. If we take the time, we won't be left in want. But he also wants us to know that our rewards are not just in this life. In fact, they are primarily in the next. Even as you read this, he is preparing a place for you.

God, who knows your heart better than any other, eagerly awaits the day when you will see him. He knows that his kingdom and his presence will satisfy your every longing. He is cheering you on as you endure on earth, and he is beyond eager to welcome you into your eternal home. One day in his coming kingdom is better than a thousand in your dream vacation spot. May you catch a glimpse of this today and may it strengthen you in your walk.

Father, encourage me with all that is to come so I might run well in this life. Thank you that you are preparing a place for me to be with you forever!

Thoughts on Beauty

Your beauty should not come from outward adornment, such as elaborate hairstyles and the wearing of gold jewelry or fine clothes. Rather, it should be that of your inner self, the unfading beauty of a gentle and quiet spirit, which is of great worth in God's sight.

1 PETER 3:3-4 NIV

God's thoughts on beauty are so contrary to the world's. Often we are tempted to let Hollywood or contemporary magazines define beauty instead of the Word of God.

In a world that so emphasizes outward appearance, flawless perfection, and unattainable standards, how awesome to know God values a beauty the world knows so little about. He sees the beauty inside each of us. We have beauty that can't be sold in a department store or on a trendy website. Our beauty can radiate from within because his Spirit is at work in us.

Lord, help me to see myself the way you do. Help me to recognize the beauty you have placed within me. Teach me to be gentle in all that I do and to walk in the quietness of a spirit full of beauty.

A WILLING HEART

Restore to me the joy of your salvation,
and make me willing to obey you.
PSALM 51:12 NLT

Picture a defiant little girl, crying in the timeout chair. All she has to do to be welcomed back is admit she drew on the wall, or apologize for hitting her brother, or eat the carrots. But she doesn't. She won't. She can't. Unwilling to accept her parent's entirely reasonable conditions, she wallows in her sadness. We're grownups now, but sometimes we find ourselves in that same corner. Bound by our own rebellious choices, we pull our knees up to our chests and wallow.

Yes, we heard God's direction, but we didn't feel like following. We don't *like* carrots. Bobby *deserved* it. It is our choice, always, to stay in the chair and it's our choice, always, to get up and rejoin the party. God restores us, forgives us, and he can even make us willing—if we can admit that we need his help.

Lord, I confess it. That little girl is me. Rebellious and defiant, I ignore your will and exercise my own. Though exhilarating in the moment, my rebellion robs me of my joy. Restore me, God, to the joy of your salvation. Your way is best, and your will is perfect. Please help me remain there, Father, always.

Cultivating Kindness

Be kind and compassionate to one another, forgiving each other, just as in Christ God forgave you.
EPHESIANS 4:32 NIV

Life isn't always kind to us. Sometimes circumstances are difficult and trying. The people we interact with on a daily basis, some close and others not so close, can at times be harsh, unloving, or downright mean. Yet the Word of God gives us instruction to treat others with kindness and compassion regardless of how they treat us.

Being kind to others doesn't always come naturally—especially if we have been treated poorly. It can be very freeing to look for creative ways to be kind. As we begin to make conscious choices to be kind and loving, it can become a way of life. We need to forgive people on a heart level, whether forgiveness is ever asked for or not. The kind of freedom forgiveness brings has no equal. When we walk in kindness, compassion, and forgiveness, we are being obedient to his Word.

Lord, help me to always walk in kindness, compassion, and love. Help me to be quick to forgive just as you forgave me.

You're Rich... No, Really!

Tell them to use their money to do good. They should be rich in good works and generous to those in need, always being ready to share with others. By doing this they will be storing up their treasure as a good foundation for the future so that they may experience true life.

1 TIMOTHY 6:18-19 NLT

We have been so richly blessed. With the many things that call for our attention and money, it is sometimes easy to pass by opportunities to help and bless others in need. Yet the Word of God instructs us to be generous and ready to share with others.

In doing so, we not only will be storing up treasure, it is a way in which we can experience true life. What a promise!

Father, help me to be generous with all you have given me. Help me to share freely with those in need.

NO SURPRISES

Beloved, do not be surprised at the fiery trial when it comes upon you to test you, as though something strange were happening to you.
1 PETER 4:12 ESV

Strange things happen sometimes. If they happened often they wouldn't be strange. Getting into a car accident is strange, running into someone you haven't seen in twenty years is strange, having a hot air balloon land in your backyard is strange. When strange things happen, we post pictures about the event, tell the story over and over, and if it's really strange perhaps the local news will cover the story.

Facing a fiery trial as a Christian isn't strange. Peter tells us not to be surprised at the trials we face as though something strange were happening to us. Fiery trials are commonplace for Christians. They're not eye-grabbing headlines that seem way out of the ordinary. The purpose of these trials is testing. God tests us. He doesn't test us with a sinister grin hoping we fail. He tests us while giving us the ultimate cheat sheet, shouting from the front row and cheering us on.

God, help me persevere through the trials I face today. I want to continue in confidence, knowing and believing that you are good.

HELP ME GET DRESSED

God has chosen you and made you his holy people. He loves you. So you should always clothe yourselves with mercy, kindness, humility, gentleness, and patience.

COLOSSIANS 3:12 NCV

The classic nightmare we've all had at one time or another involves us forgetting to have properly dressed ourselves before going out in public. Everyone sees our state of immodesty and laughs. Hopefully we wake up before the dream goes on much longer.

Starting any day without putting on the characteristics in this Scripture may well produce the same result of embarrassment. Compassion, kindness, humility, gentleness, and patience don't put themselves on us. We put them on with the help of the Holy Spirit. Pride, arrogance, impatience, and judgment will rise up in our lives if we're not properly dressed. The results will damage our relationships and put us in a place we wish we could wake up from.

Father God, today I ask that by the power of your Spirit you would put in me a compassionate heart, kindness, humility, gentleness, and patience. Be glorified through me today.

READY TO FORGIVE

Be gentle and ready to forgive; never hold grudges. Remember, the Lord forgave you, so you must forgive others.

COLOSSIANS 3:13 TLB

The Bible never really labors over the details when it comes to us forgiving one another. The commands to do so are generally short, to the point, and void of any comfort to those who opt not to forgive. It's natural and healthy, to a degree, to be angry when you or someone you love has been violated. Some people feel so guilty about being angry that they never get to the point of forgiving. Some think they need to hold onto a grudge to protect themselves from being hurt again.

Jesus tells us we must forgive. That is to validate the fact that wrong was committed. There's never need to feel bad about being angry over a legitimate violation. But there's also no room to withhold forgiveness from the one who wronged you.

Lord you've forgiven me. Help me see and remember that. Give me grace to forgive those who've wronged me.

REJOICE

To the degree that you share the sufferings of Christ, keep on rejoicing, so that also at the revelation of His glory you may rejoice with exultation.

1 PETER 4:13 NASB

Athletes have heard the phrase: "Sweat in training or bleed in the game." Without putting your best effort into practice, the results in the arena will be humiliating and painful. The choice is to do the hard work when nobody is watching and get rewarded when the stands are full, or take short cuts in practice and endure the scorn of your audience.

The Christian life is much the same. In this life we face trials with joy, we embrace discipline and limitations for the sake of loving God and our neighbors, we think of others' wellbeing before our own. We give when it hurts and we find it very satisfying. Christians who live this way haven't lost their marbles. They know what Peter said is true. God's glory will be revealed when he returns. Until then, we rejoice!

Jesus, give me vision for the day you will return. Give me a picture of your coming glory.

CONSIDER THE SPARROWS

"Look at the birds of the air; they neither sow nor reap nor gather into barns, and yet your heavenly Father feeds them. Are you not of more value than they? And can any of you by worrying add a single hour to your span of life?"
MATTHEW 6:26-27 NRSV

Jesus told those he taught when faced with the worries of this life to consider the sparrows. Jesus alongside his Father created the sparrows as well as the whole earth that sustains the life of sparrows. When he used them as an example to believers, he didn't just come up with the comparison the night before during his sermon preparation. Jesus created those sparrows thousands of years before he taught. With every ounce of intent at the point of creation, he foresaw the day he would make this point through them.

Sparrows were designed to make beautiful sounds, to bring joy to those who watched and listened to them, and to show children of God how to live. Sparrows wake up knowing that worms will come to the surface. They fetch what they need for the day, carelessly soar around for no apparent reason, then find some more worms and grubs when they're hungry. They go to sleep with total trust that tomorrow will be no less delightful than today.

God, thank you for sparrows that show us how to live. Help us live in total trust of you today!

HELP ME SEE PAST ME!

Since there is jealousy and quarreling among you,
are you not worldly?
1 CORINTHIANS 3:3 NIV

Jealousy destroys relationships and it demonstrates a value
system that isn't in line with God's kingdom. When your focus is
predominately on yourself, you'll quickly find jealousy rising up in
your heart on every turn. You'll notice what some people have that
you don't—you may even have accusations built up in your heart
about how they got what they have illegitimately.

What's the alternative? Recognize God has given you all that you
have and be content. Realize you don't know all that goes on in the
lives of those you're tempted to be jealous of. Pray that God gives you
a sincere heart of love toward them. Rejoice in the success of others
and genuinely grieve with their losses.

God, move my heart to care for others rather than be overly
concerned with myself. Move my heart from jealousy to
wisdom and contentment.

Our Creator

When I look at the night sky and see the work of your fingers—
the moon and the stars you set in place—
what are mere mortals that you should think about them,
human beings that you should care for them?
Yet you made them only a little lower than God
and crowned them with glory and honor.

PSALM 8:3-5 NLT

Skydiving looks absolutely thrilling and completely terrifying.
Those who have had the courage to leap from a plane say it is an
exhilarating experience that cannot be replicated. A woman shared
that as she floated through the air, praise welled up in her soul as she
saw God's magnificent creation from a completely new viewpoint.
The psalmist was just as enthralled with the mighty works of God
and in awe of the fact that God could stoop to even notice or care
about mere mortals. God created man is his very own image with a
coronation of sorts as he crowned him with glory and honor and gave
him dominion over the earth.

Are you feeling somewhat insignificant this morning and maybe a
bit forgotten? Consider this: you are fearfully and wonderfully made!
Your value cannot be measured. Through the vast splendor of the
universe, God sees you, he thinks about you, and he cares for you.
Revel in that for a moment.

Oh God, it is amazing that you, the God of the universe, care
about me! You have fashioned me in your image for a divine
purpose. Help me to live in the wonder of this truth.

Praise the Lord!

Let all that I am praise the LORD.
I will praise the LORD as long as I live.
I will sing praises to my God with my dying breath.
> PSALM 146:1-2 NLT

God commands us numerous times in his Word to praise him. How can he expect us to fulfill such a directive? On some days, digging through the rubble to find a nugget to be thankful for is flat out formidable. Negative thoughts can float through the mind like a shadowy cloud, and if allowed to remain, can darken the entire day.

The psalmist understood. Even though his life was in constant danger, he knew that as he centered on the greatness of God, his problems would be divinely solved. He wasn't engrossed in his own stuff. He looked at God and saw him for who he was: a helper, creator, promise keeper, provider, deliverer, healer, protector, and defender. Make David's words your prayer to the Lord. As you do, your heart will nod "yes" and hope will arise.

Lord, you are great and worthy to be praised! I lift my voice in praise and thanksgiving this morning. Blessed be your name.

TUG-OF-WAR

If you direct your heart rightly,
you will stretch out your hands toward him.
If iniquity is in your hand, put it far away,
and do not let wickedness reside in your tents.
Surely then you will lift up your face without blemish;
you will be secure, and will not fear.
JOB 11:13-15 NRSV

If you hang around kids at all, you will soon observe a fair amount of selfish behavior. They pay no attention to a certain toy until another child starts playing with it, and then it becomes a tug-of-war. In their immaturity, they focus on their own happiness without regard for anyone else's. Wouldn't you agree that sometimes when we don't get what we want, we act like children?

Are you in the middle of a tug-of-war with God this morning? Are you bucking and bristling at the circumstances he has allowed? The best decision you could make as you start your day is to surrender—lay down your own desires and demands and let God have his way. He loves you too much to let you have your way because he knows his way is better for you. There is nothing like the peace of surrender.

Lord, this morning I surrender myself anew to you. Forgive me for my willfulness. I put aside my selfish agenda that contends with your plan for me. Thank you for loving me so much!

RANSOMED

I will shout for joy and sing your praises,
for you have ransomed me.

PSALM 71:23 NLT

A boy whittled a little boat out of a scrap of wood. Proud of himself for his accomplishment, he decided to test it out in a stream that wound through his family's property. He ran alongside the boat on the bank, watching it bob through the water. Soon the current picked up, and away his boat went...faster than he could follow. Weeks later, as he and his dad were in town, they spied his little boat in the window of a store with a price tag on it! With joy he ran into the shop expecting to retrieve his lost boat. But no, he would have to pay for it. In the end, the boy earned enough money to buy back what was already his.

Isn't that what Christ did for us? He made us, lost us, and then bought us back, paying for us with his life. The psalmist couldn't contain his joy as he contemplated that wonder! God has ransomed us. On this fine morning, remember to thank God for redeeming you. Shout for joy and sing his praises!

Oh, Lord, you created me, but I was lost in sin until you found me. Thank you for buying me back! Blessed be your holy name.

Stop It!

Don't worry about anything; instead, pray about everything.
Tell God what you need, and thank him for all he has done.
Then you will experience God's peace, which exceeds anything
we can understand. His peace will guard your hearts and minds
as you live in Christ Jesus.

PHILIPPIANS 4:6-7 NLT

Worry, stress, and tension are some of the most crippling and
destructive forces we face. Satan uses them against us to render us
ineffective and unproductive. Worry is an agitation clothed in fear,
and if left unchecked, it can deepen into anxiety and depression. God
understands these tendencies, so he has provided us with a solution:
stop it! Instead, *pray*. Pray about everything. When we do, God's
peace—the kind that transcends understanding and stands guard over
our hearts and minds—will settle into our souls.

Don't let this day begin with one single worry! Tell God all about it
and surrender it to him. You will be amazed that the burden will lift
and peace will descend.

Lord, forgive me for my unbelief that is working itself out in
worry. I give you my concerns and receive the peace that you
promise to give me. Thank you for all you have done.

THE ANCIENT PATH

Stand by the roads, and look,
and ask for the ancient paths,
where the good way is; and walk in it,
and find rest for your souls.
JEREMIAH 6:16 ESV

Some of us are fascinated by remnants from the past: a ramshackle cabin, a collapsing silo, an overgrown garden, a decaying fence—the shadows of lives long gone. Sights like these can stir a yearning, a wistfulness, almost a pining, to know something more of the living that occurred at that place. Others are taken only with the present. They live on the cutting edge of all things new and there is not a nostalgic bone in their bodies. Different kinds of people with different outlooks, and in the natural life both are just fine.

In our spiritual walk, however, it seems that God is taken more with the past. Jeremiah tells us to stop at the crossroads and take in the view before making a choice. In one direction lies the road of worldly thinking. In the other, the old, good, and godly way. Do you have a decision to make today? Look to the ancient Book: it's old but just as relevant and perfect as the day it was written. Follow its direction and you will find peace.

Lord, guide me today as I face decisions that will impact my life and those around me. Give me discernment and the courage to walk on your path.

THE DO-OVER

The faithful love of the LORD never ends!
His mercies never cease.
Great is his faithfulness;
his mercies begin afresh each morning.
LAMENTATIONS 3:22-23 NLT

Have you ever looked back over segments of your life and wished you could have a "do over"? As time has gone by, you have gained a new perspective on the past. It is easy to see the folly of a decision and grieve over wrong-doing. The vivid memories of your past sins and failures are tough to erase, and even though you know God has forgiven you, you have not forgiven yourself. This is the spot where Satan wants you to camp.

Let's consider the Lord's view of your predicament. First, he sees you as forgiven and has forgotten your sins. In addition to forgetting your past failures, his love and mercy never stop. They begin fresh every morning. Jump in the shower of God's love and mercy this morning, and remember, every twenty-four hours, you get to have a do-over!

Jesus, I receive your faithful love and mercy this morning. Yesterday is gone forever and I will live today bathed in your mercies.

TWO ARE BETTER

Two people are better off than one, for they can help each other succeed. If one person falls, the other can reach out and help. But someone who falls alone is in real trouble. Likewise, two people lying close together can keep each other warm. But how can one be warm alone?

ECCLESIASTES 4:9-11 NLT

Sharing our struggles with others is never easy. No one likes to admit to feeling weak, lost, or broken. Instead of turning to those who could help us when we are struggling, we foolishly attempt to cover up what we are wrestling with. This only leads to isolation and a deeper place of pain. Depending on others for help is not a sign of weakness. God gave us each other for support, encouragement, understanding, and unity.

We all have our times of need, and being vulnerable with others is critical. It is in our vulnerability that we can see the beauty of friendship. True friends don't leave you alone in your struggles; they enter into your battles, fight alongside you, and pick you up when you feel too weak to go another step. They exemplify God's love for you. If you find yourself this morning in a place of weakness, seek out a friend. Refuse to hide in your struggles.

Jesus, thank you for friends that I can be real, honest, and open with. Thank you for those who can help carry me through the hard times in life.

THE GREATEST COMMANDMENT

"'Love the Lord your God with all your heart and with all
your soul and with all your mind.' This is the first and greatest
commandment."

MATTHEW 22:37 NIV

If you were raised in church, you may remember being told that
Jesus loved you, and you must love him too. It sounded so simple
and in a beautifully childish way, you loved God. Now as an adult,
the words may still roll off the tongue easily, but how is it really
done? Obedience necessarily involves every part of our being: mind,
will, and emotion. Our love for God should be reflected in our
thoughts, speech, relationships, behavior, the way we dress, and the
entertainment we choose.

Loving God with this level of intensity cannot be done on our own.
The power to live it out comes from God himself. He loved us first!
Ask God for a new understanding of his love for you this morning and
determine that you will love him back with everything that is in you.

Jesus, thank you for loving me with a love that cannot be
measured. I want to love you back with my whole being. Help
me to show my love for you in everything I do today.

AUGUST

O give thanks to the LORD,
for he is good,
for his steadfast love endures forever.

PSALM 136:1 NRSV

GOD'S PROMISES

Don't be afraid, for I am with you.
Don't be discouraged, for I am your God.
I will strengthen you and help you.
I will hold you up with my victorious right hand.
ISAIAH 41:10 NLT

God's Word is full of wonderful promises that are often conditional: a command and a promise. Think of the parent who says to their child, "Eat all your vegetables, and I will give you some ice cream." The child is motivated to obey by the tantalizing promise. Isaiah speaks to us as God's children, challenging us to embrace God's offer of help and strength by meeting his conditions. He will give strength, help, and keep us from sinking if we refuse fear and discouragement. As we embrace the truth that God is ever present, powerful, and loving, we are then in a position to receive the promises he offers.

How is your outlook for this new day? Are you discouraged and fearful about the issues you are facing? Perhaps you need to repent of unbelief and then remind yourself of who God is. Strong. Helpful. Powerful. Present.

Lord, I love your promises, and I want to experience every one of them. Help me to uphold my part of the bargain. I'm sorry for my unbelief, fear, and discouragement. I choose to place my complete confidence in you this day.

TRANSFERRED AND TRANSFORMED

He has rescued us from the kingdom of darkness and transferred us into the Kingdom of his dear Son, who purchased our freedom and forgave our sins.

COLOSSIANS 1:13-14 NLT

If you've ever traveled to a foreign country, you have probably experienced culture shock to some degree. Feelings of confusion and anxiety are common as you encounter a way of life completely different from your own. You've been transferred from one society to another.

Colossians speaks of a different sort of relocation—not a physical one but a spiritual one. Through Christ's forgiveness we have been rescued from a life ruled by Satan's power and transferred to a completely new realm—to the kingdom under the headship of a loving Savior. This transference is much greater than a mere change of location; it is a transformation of our character. We aren't where we once were and we aren't who we once were. Take a few minutes this morning to praise God for rescuing you from darkness and giving you new life in a brand new land!

Lord, my heart is full of thanksgiving this morning for the miracle of transformation. Thank you for rescuing me from my sin and shame and giving me eternal life.

A Broken Heart

The LORD is near to the brokenhearted
and saves the crushed in spirit.
    PSALM 34:18 ESV

Goodbyes are possibly one of the most difficult challenges we face—whether through death or a major move. Loving deeply is costly. The price Jesus paid for loving was death. He understands the pain of separation—his own Father forsook him when he took on the sins of the world. But now he is at the right hand of the Father as our intercessor and high priest who understands our weaknesses. He knows what it's like to have a broken heart and he rescues us.

In the course of ordinary life, there are times when we experience heartbreak for any number of reasons. It is comforting to know that Jesus understands because he has been there. Be reminded this morning that he is especially close to you and will rescue your bruised spirit. Cry out to him—his ear is inclined your way!

Lord, I am so grateful that you identify with my pain. Thank you for your nearness. Help me to keep trusting you until relief comes.

FAITH WITHOUT SIGHT

It was by faith that Abraham obeyed when God called him to leave home and go to another land that God would give him as his inheritance. He went without knowing where he was going.

HEBREWS 11:8 NLT

Abraham, the father of the faithful, was a man of obedience. Had he heard God's call, but out of fear or unbelief disregarded it, God could not have established a new nation through his descendants. Abraham took the risk because he was convinced that God was true, and set out for a place he did not know. Genuine faith always obeys God... in fact, our obedience to God is the indication that our faith is real. Abraham took one step at a time before the next one was revealed.

This morning you may be following the Lord as though in the dark. You just don't see where he is leading you. Remember that he sees the entire picture and is engineering the circumstances of your life very carefully. He knows what he is doing and asks that you just take one step of faith at a time.

O Lord, I come to you this morning to reaffirm my faith in you. You are good, loving, and faithful, and you love me too much to leave me directionless. Help me to trust you more and lead me in the way everlasting.

BLIND TRUST

You love him even though you have never seen him; though not seeing him, you trust him; and even now you are happy with the inexpressible joy that comes from heaven itself. And your further reward for trusting him will be the salvation of your souls.

I PETER 1:8-9 TLB

Is it possible to love and trust a person you have never seen? Peter seemed to think so. Writing to Christians during a time of great persecution under the tyrant Nero, Peter reminded them of their faith and love for a God they had never laid eyes on. Peter and the other apostles had the privilege of experiencing Jesus firsthand, but these folks' trust transcended the natural, and with eyes of faith they experienced the inexpressible joy of their salvation.

How are you doing in the "blind trust" department? Does God seem distant and indifferent on this fine morning? Remember that although you cannot see God with your physical eyes, he is very much with you. His eyes are on you and his ears are open to your cries. Trust him today. The reward for trusting him will be the salvation of your souls.

Jesus, it would be so wonderful to sit down for a cup of tea with you in person so we could chat about all the things I'm concerned about right now. But Lord, I know you are real even though I cannot see you with my physical eyes. Thank you for being with me.

CONTENTED STRENGTH

Not that I am speaking of being in need, for I have learned in whatever situation I am to be content. I know how to be brought low, and I know how to abound. In any and every circumstance, I have learned the secret of facing plenty and hunger, abundance and need. I can do all things through him who strengthens me.

PHILIPPIANS 4:11-13 NIT

Paul was a man who knew how to survive and thrive in just about any situation. He had been whipped, lashed, beaten, stoned, shipwrecked, lost, imprisoned, hungry, thirsty, and cold. Yet, in spite of it all, he had learned the secret of living contentedly by fully trusting in Christ, who gave him strength.

Our problems are small in comparison but still significant to us and to God. Remember, your God would never ask something of you that he would not supply the necessary strength to accomplish. This morning, know that whatever is ahead for you, you can rest in knowing that Christ's strength is enough to see you through—not just barely squeaking by, but with contentment!

Thank you, Lord, for sharing Paul's secret with us. Help me to be content with my present, and to fully rely on the strength you promise to provide. I can do everything because I have you.

DEER FEET

The Sovereign LORD is my strength;
he makes my feet like the feet of a deer,
he enables me to tread on the heights.
HABAKKUK 3:19 NIV

When God created deer, he gave them feet that would enable them to do everything they needed to do. From galloping across an open field at 30-35 mph to clearing an 8-foot fence, to scrambling up a steep embankment, they are amazingly athletic. The strength for forward motion comes from their muscular hind legs. We are not deer, but certainly need that kind of muscle in our inner self. How are we to navigate the unexpected sharp turns in life and have the agility to maneuver through life's difficulties? Only by the strength of our powerful, sovereign, and present God. The journey of life is often steep and slippery, but our goal is heaven, where we will forever tread in heavenly places with Christ.

Your God, almighty and victorious, is your strength today. He will give you what it takes to walk with him through the valleys and mountains. He will make you sure-footed!

Thanks, God, for giving me strength and confidence that my steps are ordered by you and you will not let me fall. Hold me up when I hit the icy patches and guide me by your wonderful hand.

FIX YOUR THOUGHTS

Fix your thoughts on what is true, and honorable, and right, and pure, and lovely, and admirable. Think about things that are excellent and worthy of praise.

PHILIPPIANS 4:8 NLT

A 4-year-old girl complained repeatedly of boredom. Her mom countered by relating all they had done that day but could not convince her daughter otherwise. The complaints continued. When mom repeated her case, little girl said emphatically, "You can't control my mind!" How true. No one can manage our thinking but ourselves. Thoughts can be corralled and managed—it's not an easy task, but we can focus our thoughts. In fact, we must! Filling our minds with the truth of God's Word will help us dwell on good things, and give us the ability to identify any untruths.

Begin your day today with God's truth, and reject any thought that does not line up with it. Believe you are loved, you are cared for, and God will never leave you. Think on the things that are excellent and worthy of praise.

Lord, I choose today to fix my thoughts on you and to believe you are a God of your Word. Help me to gather my wayward thoughts and surrender them to you.

Forgetting

I focus on this one thing: Forgetting the past and looking forward to what lies ahead, I press on to reach the end of the race and receive the heavenly prize for which God, through Christ Jesus, is calling us.

PHILIPPIANS 3:13-14 NLT

Have you ever rushed to the next room for an important task and found yourself standing in the doorway, wondering why in the world you were there? Forgetting things can be a considerable annoyance. In our spiritual lives, however, forgetting is a must! If we don't, we'll get bogged down in memories of past sins and failings, or try to live on the blessings and achievements of the past. Paul didn't look back. Nothing was going to deter him from receiving the heavenly prize that lay ahead.

Put your past behind you. Christ has. He has cancelled out your sin and removed it from your life and from his memory. Continue your journey toward your heavenly prize with abandon!

Lord, thank you for forgiving me of my past and giving me new life in you. I choose today to forgive myself and to look forward to all you have planned for me.

FORGIVENESS

"If you do not forgive others, then your Father will not forgive your transgressions."
MATTHEW 6:15 NASB

Forgiveness is the necessary path for the Christian. Having begun our new life through Christ's forgiveness, we must then offer the same to others. 1 Samuel 24 tells a story of how David lived out this principle in his life. He and his men were hiding in the back of a cave, when his pursuer, King Saul, walked in. Here was David's opportunity to finally be freed from his pursuer, but he could not harm him. He merely cut off a piece of his garment as proof that there was no vengeance in his heart.

Sometimes it is hard to forgive others for fear that what they have done will be minimized somehow and that they won't be held to account. Remember, it is not our place to hold court. God will one day judge all actions; in the meantime, forgive, so that the life and joy of Jesus can reign. Make this your prayer today.

Jesus, I confess to you that I have held anger and judgment in my heart. Please forgive me as I forgive my offender. Thank you, Lord, for the freedom there is in forgiveness.

TEMPTATION

Because he himself has suffered when tempted, he is able to
help those who are being tempted.
HEBREWS 2:18 ESV

Because of our humanity, we will be tempted to sin in many different
ways—for our entire lives. Jesus himself faced temptation from Satan
when he walked the earth. You shouldn't feel guilty about the stuff
that tempts you; it isn't you that is tempting yourself. We know that
Satan is the tempter and his job is to walk around enticing mankind to
violate God's laws in numerous ways. He even tried his tactics on Jesus.

If you are feeling an onslaught of temptation, follow Jesus's model and
pray to your heavenly Father who will hear you. God's heart is toward
you when you are tempted, and he wants you to ask him for help.

Father, thank you that your heart is for me, both when I am
tempted and when I sin. Please remind me and give me the
grace to call on your name when I am being tempted that I
might find the strength to resist.

CHOSEN BY GOD

You have been chosen by God himself—you are priests of the King, you are holy and pure, you are God's very own—all this so that you may show to others how God called you out of the darkness into his wonderful light.

1 PETER 2:9 TLB

The world loves to define us. If we aren't careful and we accept those definitions as our own, they can dictate our lives and determine how we feel about ourselves. Often we believe what the world tells us about who we are: our jobs determine how successful we are, and our relationships determine how valued we are. Even our zip code can determine our worth. These definitions aren't life giving; they destroy our confidence and confuse our self-worth.

Thankfully, the Lord doesn't measure our value with the same scales the world uses. He calls us loved and worthy simply because we are his. Because we belong to him, we are given a unique and special identity. Though we can feel insignificant in the world's eyes, in God's we are treasured and priceless.

Lord, help me to always put my value in your hands. Thank you for loving me more than I can imagine. Help me to ignore all the definitions others have of me, and instead embrace the identity you have graciously given me.

HE IS ENOUGH

He said to me, "My grace is sufficient for you, for my power is made perfect in weakness." Therefore I will boast all the more gladly about my weaknesses, so that Christ's power may rest on me.

2 CORINTHIANS 12:9 NIV

The doctor, a wise and devout Christian, listened compassionately as his patient's story unfolded. The woman's husband was gravely ill and she was struggling emotionally and physically as she faced each day without much hope for the future. Then he said something that both alarmed and encouraged her. "You know, if your husband should die, you will be okay. You have Jesus."

Are you remembering that you have Jesus this morning? Today may have dawned bright and sunny, but inside all is not well in your world, and the next twenty-four hours look unrelentingly gloomy. Pull yourself up. If you know Christ, you know that his grace is sufficient, his strength is made perfect in your weakness, and his presence sustains you. You are standing on solid ground, immovable and unchanging. Christ has a grip on you—cling to him and know that he is enough!

Lord, help me today. My faith is wavering and I am unmotivated to persevere. I know your grace is sufficient for me and your power can work in my weakness. I trust you in this moment. You are enough.

HE UNDERSTANDS

Have you never heard?
Have you never understood?
The Lord is the everlasting God,
the Creator of all the earth.
He never grows weak or weary.
No one can measure the depths of his understanding.
ISAIAH 40:28 NLT

There is something in us that longs to be understood. When tragedy suddenly strikes—financial difficulties or a devastating loss—we need someone to identify with us and offer more than just platitudes. We long for the comforting word or the shoulder to lean on from someone who has been there. People join support groups for this reason: they can communicate with others who have had similar experiences.

It would be a sad day indeed if Isaiah had not given us an answer to this dilemma. God knows exactly what we are going through and he understands. He will never tire of offering his unlimited strength and comfort in answer to our prayers. Look to him today, rather than to others.

Oh, God, I am so grateful that you understand me. You created me, you know me better than anyone else, and you love me more than I can imagine. Thank you for never tiring of me and understanding me fully.

HOPE IN GOD

So, Lord, where do I put my hope?
My only hope is in you.
   PSALM 39:7 NLT

It was a day like every other. The lame man arrived with the help of
his family to spend his waking hours begging at the temple gate.
Crippled from birth, it was about the only thing he could do to
survive. It was 3:00 p.m.—the last formal prayer time of the day when
the Jews would make their sacrifices and often give alms to the poor.
As Peter and John arrived at the gate, the lame man asked for money,
hoping for a coin or two. Imagine his utter amazement when Peter
said, "I don't have any silver or gold for you. But I'll give you what
I have. In the name of Jesus Christ the Nazarene, get up and walk!"
(See Acts 3:6.)

Are you sitting at that gate this morning, hoping you will receive a bit
of joy or encouragement from someone passing by? Remember this.
No human being can meet your needs—only God can. Are you placing
your hope horizontally rather than vertically? The lame man "looked
up" and received much more than he ever dreamed. This day, put your
hope in God.

Lord, today I choose to put my hope in you as you are the
source of everything I need. Forgive me for looking elsewhere
and help me to keep my eyes on you.

In His Image

I will make a mortal more rare than fine gold,
A man more than the golden wedge of Ophir.
ISAIAH 13:12 NKJV

What do you consider to be your most valuable possession? Is it your bank account, your car, your home, or your cabin on the lake? On a less superficial level, you might say your family, friends, your church, or your job. If we asked the God of the universe the same question (and remember he owns it all!), he would say, "You!" Think about that for a minute. God created you in his very own image. You are not God, but you possess similar qualities, not unlike a skilled artist who paints a self-portrait. The portrait is not the artist himself, but an exact likeness.

Today you may feel neglected, unnoticed, and even insignificant. Remember this: you are of infinite value. You were created to love, to have a relationship with God and others, to think, reason, feel, and create. Your potential is limitless. You are a mortal more rare than fine gold. Believe it!

Lord, I am in awe of your incredible love for me. Thank you for creating me in your image with no price tag high enough to match my worth. I want to live this day displaying the wonder of your glory. You are worthy!

My Guide

I will lead the blind by a way they do not know,
In paths they do not know I will guide them.
I will make darkness into light before them
And rugged places into plains.
These are the things I will do,
And I will not leave them undone.

ISAIAH 42:16 NASB

God's people, the Israelites, had been in captivity for seventy years, and now at long last, they desperately needed a guide to lead them back home. It was as if they were blind, having no idea of which direction to take. God promised to remove the obstacles in their way and shine a light on their journey.

Our lives, too, are a pilgrimage through uncharted territory. So many have walked the path before us, but our steps on a similar path can feel like a walk in the dark. Maybe you are on a course with obstacles that seem insurmountable. Perhaps the path you planned for your life looked much different. You need a guide—a loving, good, and compassionate guide—to lead you on your journey home. You have one. He is a wonderful counselor, mighty God, everlasting Father, and the Prince of Peace. Trust him today.

Thank you, Lord, for your promise to be my guide through the dark and rugged places. Although I cannot see my way clearly, you can and will walk closely by my side. You are my loving and good God.

PUT ON YOUR BELT

Stand firm then, with the belt of truth buckled around your waist, with the breastplate of righteousness in place.
EPHESIANS 6:14 NIV

Every single day, court is in session all over our country. The ultimate goal of the process is to discern the truth. The truth discovered may set the defendant free, or send him to jail. There is power in truth, but also power in the enemy's deception. Wearing the belt of truth enables us to discern between the two. For the Roman soldier, the belt was the home for his sword. It held up his heavy breastplate and provided a place to tuck in his tunic to keep him from tripping. The truth of God's Word does that for us spiritually. It can be wielded like a sword against the deception of the enemy, and it can keep us from falling into sin. The Word holds us together.

Have you put on your belt of truth today? Spend some time in God's Word and soak in the truth found there. Don't rely on any other source to guide you. Stand firm in the truth!

Lord, I am so grateful that you have provided the standard of absolute and unfailing truth for my life. I put on the belt this morning and look forward to a joy-filled and victorious day.

SLIPPING

I cried out, "I am slipping!"
but your unfailing love, O LORD, supported me.
When doubts filled my mind,
your comfort gave me renewed hope and cheer.
PSALM 94:18-19 NLT

If you live in the northern part of our country where ice and snow abound, you probably have slipped and fallen at least once. As you know, it happens quickly! You are bustling along when suddenly out go your feet and down you go. After assessing for injury, you quickly look around to see if you had any observers. It is humiliating to be so out of control.

Life can sometimes blindside us with difficulties that completely throw us off balance. And, yes, it can be humbling to realize that we do not have control over much of life. Without God's support, we will take a tumble. Satan's plan for us is to slip and fall into anger, fear, depression, and unbelief. Cry out to God this morning; hang on to him tightly, and he will keep you from falling.

This morning, Lord, I cry out to you for support. I am unsure if I can keep my feet under me as I deal with this unexpected circumstance. Thank you that your comfort will give me renewed hope.

THE GOD OF ALL COMFORT

Praise be to the God and Father of our Lord Jesus Christ, the Father of compassion and the God of all comfort.

2 CORINTHIANS 1:3 NIV

Comfort is what our hearts cry out for in times of trouble or sorrow. We need someone to sit beside us, listen to our story, put a comforting arm around our shoulders, and just be there. Our friends and families, though they love us, are limited by time and resources. They cannot always meet our needs. This is the moment to look to God—the source of compassion and comfort. Read the Psalms and hang on to the promises found there. God does not grow tired or weary of us; he is always near.

Have a great day today—yes, even joyful! You have a God who loves you. He is full of compassion and is the source of all comfort. Run to him this morning and let him soothe your troubled soul.

Father, you are my God—full of compassion and eager to comfort my soul. I give you my distresses and ask that you would bind up my heart. I begin this day with your strength.

WAIT FOR THE LORD

I wait for the LORD, my soul waits,
and in his word I hope;
my soul waits for the Lord
more than watchmen for the morning,
more than watchmen for the morning.

PSALM 130:5-6 ESV

We live in a fast culture. Instant messaging, fast food, high speed Internet, automated everything! The quicker, the shorter, the better we like it. Waiting is just not on our list of favorite things to do. We are used to getting things done in a relatively efficient fashion, yet when we pray, God seems to be on an entirely different timetable. He often asks us to wait. Why? Because God is more interested in developing our character than he is in instant messaging. Patience, endurance, faithfulness, and perseverance are being developed in the waiting.

Are you frustrated by unanswered prayers this morning? As you wait for God to answer your prayer, remember there is much being done behind the scenes. God is setting the stage, working in other people's lives, arranging the circumstances until just the right time. Then your answer will come. Don't be passive in the waiting; pray, read the Word, and hang on to the promises of God. You can do it!

Lord, please help me to be patient as I wait for you to move in my life. Nothing is wasted. You work everything for my good. I trust you to do what is best.

Beauty Measured

"Do not look on his appearance or on the height of his stature, because I have rejected him. For the Lord sees not as man sees: man looks on the outward appearance, but the Lord looks on the heart."

1 SAMUEL 16:7 ESV

When you catch a glimpse of yourself in the mirror, do you like what you see? Too often we are quick to criticize and judge our outward reflections. Some of us wish for longer hair, or brighter eyes, or a straighter smile. We can spend a long time wondering how others view our appearance, or comparing ourselves to models or even our closest friends.

It doesn't matter how good you look on the outside, or how well you think you measure up to others, it only matters how you are doing on the inside. God sees the entirety of you; he sees the parts of you that others don't. The beauty, the mess, and the brokenness—all tangled up inside you. He loves you despite everything he sees. The next time you look at yourself in the mirror, know that you are completely loved. You possess a beauty that can't be measured.

Jesus, help me see myself the way you see me. The next time I look at my reflection and am tempted to be critical, remind me how you look deeper than the color of my eyes and into the depths of my heart.

Don't Just Sit There

Since we have such a hope, we are very bold.
2 CORINTHIANS 3:12 NIV

Have you found yourself in a situation that you just knew wasn't right, but you were afraid to speak up? Maybe a friend was being mistreated, or a co-worker wasn't making ethical decisions? It takes a great deal of courage to stand up for what is right especially when everyone else around you is content to stay silent.

Maybe in that moment there was a great stirring of injustice in your heart, and you *had* to do something. In good conscience, you couldn't just sit there. In these situations, we don't have to be afraid. We can stand in confidence, because we don't stand alone. The very one who breathes boldness into us, is the one who stands beside us.

Jesus, thank you that I can have boldness because you promise to go before me. Please continue to remind me that you never leave me alone in fear. It is you who keeps me upright.

HEAVY BAGGAGE

"If you forgive others for their sins, your Father in heaven will also forgive you for your sins."
MATTHEW 6:14 NCV

It could have been a careless remark, another promise broken, or an ill-intentioned action clearly meant to hurt you. When we are wronged by others, especially those we love, it is easy to take deep offense and harbor bitterness. Sometimes our reaction to being hurt is to build up walls. We justify our reasons for not forgiving, and we continue to wear our pain, nursing it like a battle wound.

Bitterness is heavy baggage. While we are trying to protect ourselves from a repeat offense, carrying around resentment is actually doing us more harm. It eats up the best parts of us, and in its place anger grows rampantly. It can take a lot to surrender our pain to the Lord and look at our offender with compassion and grace. When we do, we are able to breathe deeply again. We can forgive because God showed us how. We can always go to him, knowing that he will never turn away from us.

Jesus, when I am tempted to hide in my hurt and stew in my pain, remind me how you are always kind and compassionate toward me. Help me to embrace my offender just as you graciously embrace me.

In Need of Grace

He gives more grace. Therefore it says, "God opposes the proud,
but gives grace to the humble."

JAMES 4:6 ESV

When our days are going well, it is easy to forget how dependent
we are on the Lord for his unending grace. Sure, we can be strong,
patient, kind, loving, selfless, and generous on our own accord, but
only for a short time. Eventually we are bound to run dry if we aren't
relying on God to fill us up with his goodness.

The danger of feeling so capable is that we forget our need for Jesus.
It's too tempting to let pride grow where humility should reside. If we
approach our days on a bended knee, recognizing that we need Jesus,
he will pour grace over all of our weaknesses and shortcomings. His
grace is what allows us to grow and draws us closer in relationship
with him.

God, I am sorry that sometimes I let pride take over my
complete need for you. Thank you so much for gifting me with
your unending grace. Thank you that you created me to need
you.

OPEN ARMS

Welcome one another as Christ has welcomed you, for the glory of God.

ROMANS 15:7 ESV

The next time you are at a party or a get-together, do a quick scan of the room. Chances are you will spot a woman or two on the outer edges looking nervous and uncomfortable. She probably feels out of place...maybe even lonely. Have you ever felt that way at a social event? Like everyone but you belongs? It's never fun to be on the outside looking in. Sometimes the best way to show God's love to the lonely is to open your arms and your heart to them.

Our need to feel wanted, loved, and accepted is strong. God never wants us to feel alone. He made it his mission for us to know that we are dearly loved and warmly embraced. As his children, as his friends, we belong with him. He sees us feeling sad and wants to comfort us. He wants us to know that we do indeed have a place, that we are heard, and that we are known.

Lord, help me see and love the lonely like you do. When I'm lonely, help me to feel your warm embrace. Thank you that you always welcome me into your arms.

FALLING BLESSINGS

How great is the goodness
you have stored up for those who fear you.
You lavish it on those who come to you for protection,
blessing them before the watching world.

PSALM 31:19 NLT

Like the leaves falling from the trees in their brilliant myriad of colors, the Lord has abundant and delightful blessings for you! Unlike the leaves, his blessings don't fall in only one season; he lavishes them on us every day.

His blessings may not look the way you expect them to; comfort, luxury, and success aren't necessarily the best things for us as they cause us to look to the world instead of to God. But he is faithfully giving everything we need for a life that glorifies his name, and we can rejoice in the testimony of his greatness. Indeed, we lack nothing when we rejoice in our salvation and the love that Jesus so greatly poured out for us.

God, your blessings are all around me, falling with beauty and grace. Thank you that you are not stingy with them, but you lavish blessing over me! Help me to recognize your blessings and give you the thanks you deserve.

NOT JUST MR. FIX IT

Enter his gates with thanksgiving
and his courts with praise;
give thanks to him and praise his name.
PSALM 100:4 NIV

How do we approach God? With love? With peace? With praise?
Or is it only with a laundry list of complaints, wants, and needs?
Sometimes we look at God as our bank account, our Mr. Fix It, or
our emotional punching bag. How many times do our prayers to God
begin with what we want, what we need, or what is going terribly
wrong in the moment?

God wants us to freely express our needs, our fears, and our hurts to
him, but that is not *all* he wants from us. We are his children. Do we
call out to him when we are experiencing deep happiness? We can
enter into his presence with more than requests and wants. We can
bring him thanksgiving and praise because he deserves it.

God, I thank you for everything good and right in my life. I am
so grateful that you love to partake in my joy and my blessings
Thank you for your presence in my life.

FOR THE SAKE OF OTHERS

Bear one another's burdens, and so fulfill the law of Christ.
GALATIANS 6:2 ESV

Close friendships and community can be beautiful—especially when life takes a challenging turn. God created us to need each other. Not only is life easier when we are able to lean on each other for emotional or practical support, but there is much joy to be found in deep and solid friendships.

God did not create us to be independent; he doesn't want us to struggle alone. He created us to serve one another, in fierce love, in relentless duty, and with soft, compassionate hearts. Do you have a friend that could use a shoulder to cry on, or an evening to share? Be available for them. In doing so, you are obeying God's ultimate desire for how we should live—for the sake of others.

Jesus, thank you that we can bear each other's burdens because ultimately it is you who bears it all. I know that others can lean on me because I can always lean on you. Help me to show love to those around me. Thank you for friends, and thank you for community.

No Longer Slaves

"If the Son sets you free, you will be free indeed."
   JOHN 8:36 NIV

As we live out our walk with Christ, we are often faced with adversity, fears, temptations, and struggles. We can become overwhelmed if we allow these fears and temptations to entrap us. We can easily forget how Jesus freed us when he died on the cross.

In Christ we are no longer slaves to the bondage of sin or the burden of fear. We are free—able to release ourselves from whatever enslaves us. We are free to roam, free to love, and free to live. Free from shame, free from guilt, free from fear, and free from bondage.

Thank you, Jesus, that in you I am a new creation. You put to death my old life. Thank you for being my Savior and rescuing me, so I can live a life of complete freedom with you.

Surrounded by Gifts

My God will supply every need of yours according to his riches in glory in Christ Jesus.
PHILIPPIANS 4:19 ESV

Blessings come in so many forms that sometimes they are hard to recognize and often taken for granted. When life turns messy and just plain hard, it is our natural inclination to focus on what is difficult or wrong in our lives. Sometimes, our current situations blind us to the little gifts in our lives. A blessing can be a sweet friend that stops by unexpectedly for a quick coffee break. Or the changing colors on an autumn day. Or a full fridge and a full pantry. A table surrounded with our favorite people breaking bread together. A restored friendship.

These blessings are all from God. He loves to delight us with beautiful and thoughtful gifts. They remind us that he sees our needs and goes above and beyond them to let us know just how much he cares.

Jesus, train my heart and my eyes to see all the gifts that you surround me with daily.

SEPTEMBER

The Lord always keeps his promises;

he is gracious in all he does.

The Lord helps the fallen

and lifts those bent beneath their loads.

PSALM 145:13-14 NLT

BREATHE AGAIN

Give all your worries to him, because he cares for you.
1 PETER 5:7 NCV

Anxiety can take our breath away. It can come in all sorts of forms: unpaid bills, a sick friend, or an uncertain future. When we are overcome with anxiety, it can paralyze us. Our entire world stops, and slowly we sink lower and lower in worry and fear. Sometimes when we feel anxious, we try to push back those feelings by eating our favorite foods, or treating ourselves to a day of shopping. Maybe we even turn to friends. But often we try to deal with anxiety alone because it can be so scary. Who could possibly understand?

God *does* understand, and he is not judging us in our struggles. If we lay our worries before him, he is quick to comfort us. The next time anxiety is pressing into you, turn to the Lord. Wash yourself in his holy Word. Allow his promises to comfort you and bring you peace.

God, when anxiety comes and threatens to paralyze me, whisper your words of comfort and promises of peace. Thank you that when I trust you, when I lean into you, I can breathe again.

PRIORITIZING RELATIONSHIP

Walk with the wise and become wise,
for a companion of fools suffers harm.
PROVERBS 13:20 NIV

Life has a way of getting busy quickly. Work, appointments, deadlines, and the list goes on. Our calendars fill up with to-do lists a mile long. Eventually something has to give; we have to prioritize. We all have a tendency to put our work ahead of our friendships. *As soon as this busy season passes, I will call my friend back. As soon as I meet this deadline, I will set up that lunch date.* But it never really happens. Days, weeks, and even months can go by because there will always be another assignment, another due date.

When we prioritize work over friends, we slowly we begin to lose our circle of support, encouragement, and voices of sensibility and reason. We need solid friendships. They are vital to us living well, and they help us make good decisions in the things that are most important. There is something so sweet about a group of friends who share life's challenges and blessings. That to-do list can wait; our friendships can't.

Dear Jesus, help me to put my friendships above my work and ambitions. Let relationships be the highest priority on my list. Thank you for your gift of friendship that enriches my life in such a beautiful way.

MY HEALER

O Lord my God, I cried to you for help,
and you have healed me.
PSALM 30:2 ESV

We all find comfort in various things. Maybe it's a good book in front
of a warm fire. Or it could be that pasta dish your mom makes. For
some it's the familiar smell of pine and the early morning mist. When
we are sick, sad, scared, or worried, we all long to be surrounded by
the people or things that comfort us. We want our needs to be seen
and taken care of in a loving and gentle way. When we face affliction,
we are desperate for a healer to come quickly.

We can always take comfort in the Lord. He loves to come and take
care of us in our weakest moments. Let him be the warm blanket
wrapped around you. Let him be the sun shining on your face. He is
the one who longs to hold you close, chase away your fears, and heal
your fevers. All you have to do is ask, and he will be there.

Jesus, thank you that you are always close, and that you make
your comforting presence known to me. Thank you that you
are my healer.

WEAPON AGAINST DOUBT

When you ask, you must believe and not doubt, because the one who doubts is like a wave of the sea, blown and tossed by the wind.

JAMES 1:6 NIV

There are periods in our life that cause us to be still, wait, and have faith in God. In those times of waiting, in the quietness, in the stillness, is often where doubt threatens to worm its way into our faith. We begin to entertain thoughts of disbelief, and wonder if God is as good as he says he is.

Faith is trusting and believing in God's goodness and faithfulness no matter how strong those doubts are. When our hearts are rooted in God, it is difficult for doubts to crack our faith. Knowing who God is, believing in his promises, and trusting his love for us is what brings us through times of wavering faith. Anchoring our trust in him silences those voices of disbelief. Remember all those times he has shown up in the midst of waiting, and use that as your weapon against doubt.

Jesus, help me to have faith in you and not in my circumstances. Thank you that even though doubts taunt me, and threaten to leave me without hope, you've made my faith in you indestructible.

INCREASED MEASURE OF FAITH

Hope deferred makes the heart sick,
but a dream fulfilled is a tree of life.
PROVERBS 13:12 NLT

When we truly hope for something, we are really putting our hearts on the line. In a time of hoping we can feel bare, exposed, and very vulnerable. Sometimes we are afraid to hope because in hoping there is always a risk—a risk of feeling let down, disappointed, or hurt. When we put our hope in people and systems, the greater the risk there is. There is no guarantee that they will fulfill our desires.

The more we put our hope in God, and not in people or circumstances, the less risk there is. Although the outcome may not always be what we initially desired, when our hope is in God, we won't be left unfulfilled or disappointed; instead, our faith is increased by his unwavering faithfulness to our hearts. He promises to carry us through every trial and challenge. He will never let our hope in him be disappointed.

Jesus, I am comforted by knowing that my hope in you will always give me an increasing measure of faith. Thank you that you give me permission to hope and dream freely.

DIFFICULT TO LOVE

Let us continue to love one another, for love comes from God.
Anyone who loves is a child of God and knows God.
1 JOHN 4:7 NLT

Have you ever encountered someone you thought would be
impossible to love? Maybe that person was critical, mean, or
overbearing. It is easy to love the people whose intentions toward us
are good. But others can be harder to embrace because we are prone
to protect ourselves.

We do have the capability in us to love everyone because we know
what it is like to be loved by God. We know how it feels to be
forgiven, to have grace poured on us daily, and to be embraced again
and again. We don't deserve to be loved so deeply, and yet we are.
And so are they. We can love others because God loves the ugliest,
meanest, and most critical parts of us. He sees beyond our mess, and
pours himself into us regardless.

Oh, God, continue to show me your love, so I can love those
around me well. Help me to share a kind word, a tenderhearted gesture, an act of service, or even a sweet embrace
with those who are more difficult to love.

NEED FOR COURAGE

Have I not commanded you? Be strong and courageous. Do not be frightened, and do not be dismayed, for the LORD your God is with you wherever you go.

JOSHUA 1:9 ESV

We all need courage. It doesn't matter if we're young or old, tall or short, confident or shy. It doesn't matter what our profession is. We could be on the frontline of a war, or in front of a classroom teaching. We all need to muster up courage to face life and its challenges head on.

Our need for courage varies. We could need courage to mend a broken relationship, to start a new job, to stand up for what is right, or to move across the country. We need courage in the most mundane parts of life and in the most risky. Whatever we do, we don't have to be afraid because God is with us. Our courage is found in the knowledge that we are never alone.

Jesus, continually teach me to cling to your truth in every situation. Show me how to stand strong and take hold of the courage that you give me. Thank you for being my strength.

DON'T BE AFRAID

"Peace I leave with you; my peace I give you. I do not give to you as the world gives. Do not let your hearts be troubled and do not be afraid."
JOHN 14:27 NIV

Watch the news for a few seconds and you'll see just how scary the world is. There is war, pain, chaos, and hatred. Add all that to our own reasons for worrying—money problems, relationships, uncertain futures—and it's enough to rob us of our sleep.

God wants to calm our spirits. He does not want us to live in fear, but in full faith that he is the ruler of the world. Regardless of the outside noise and disharmony, in God's hands is the gift of peace. Let go, relax, and breathe. He is in control in every situation even if we can't see or understand.

Thank you, Jesus, for your gift of peace. When the world is in chaos, and there are so many reasons to fear, you gently whisper not to be afraid. I am so thankful that you settle and calm my spirit.

Broken Promises

"Those the Father has given me will come to me, and I will never reject them."
JOHN 6:37 NLT

Broken promises. They hurt, don't they? When we put our hope and trust in someone, and they betray us, it is the worst kind of pain. But the reality is that we are human, and despite our best intentions, sometimes we break promises and hurt the people we love. Because of these experiences, our defenses rise, and it becomes increasingly harder to trust. We don't want to let people in or be vulnerable with anyone.

There is one we can always trust. Jesus. We don't have to push away from him for fear of rejection. He promises that he will *never* turn his face away. He will never refuse us. In a world filled with broken promises, this is a wonderful promise that will stand the test of time.

Thank you, God, that your promises weaved through your Word are not empty. They are spoken with love, given and fulfilled. Thank you that when I call out to you, you come. You always come.

EASING HEARTACHE

When he saw the crowds, he had compassion for them, because they were harassed and helpless, like sheep without a shepherd.

MATTHEW 9:36 ESV

Sometimes it is hard to know what to do when you see someone hurting. Would they accept your help? Should you intervene? Offer words of encouragement? Take their hurts and make them your own? Absolutely. The Lord wants us to show compassion for the hurting just like he showed us compassion. Take his lead. When he sees us hurting, he is moved by compassion to help.

God wants us to do whatever we can to lighten someone else's painful burdens. There are many practical ways to do this, but sometimes the best thing to do is say, "I am here, I hear you, I understand, and I am so sorry for your pain." We may not always be able to take away someone's pain, but we can certainly ease their heartache.

Jesus, show me the people around me that are hurting. Help me to show genuine love and compassion to others as you have shown to me.

OF ZERO VALUE

When the righteous cry for help, the LORD hears
and delivers them out of all their troubles.
PSALM 34:17 ESV

Do you know what holds absolutely zero value in our life but is
usually present in one way or another? Stress. What a waste of time
and emotion. When life gets chaotic and demanding, stress is bound
to rear its ugly head. Sometimes it shows up suddenly and takes away
our ability to enjoy the beautiful moments around us. It affects our
capacity to love others. And it certainly diminishes our quality of life.

When we embrace stress, we are not trusting God to help us in our
time of need. The solution to ridding our lives of stress is to call out
to the Lord when we feel it coming. We don't have to own the stress,
nor does stress need to own us; we can walk away from it and trust
that the Lord is in control. Because he is.

Jesus, when I feel stress pressing into me, thank you that I can
call out to you, and you will help me. When I let you lead my
life, you take care of all of my worries.

God's Love

May you have the power to understand, how wide, how long, how high, and how deep his love is. May you experience the love of Christ, though it is too great to understand fully. Then you will be made complete with all the fullness of life and power that comes from God.

EPHESIANS 3:18-19 NLT

There is nothing like a mother's love. It is completely self-sacrificing, patient, protective, and giving. Human love is a beautiful thing. 1 Corinthians 13 details the attributes of a love that cannot be lived out in our lives apart from the indwelling presence of the God of love.

Let your prayer today be that God would give you the power to understand the fullness of his love. Then you will begin to experience his complete love and fullness of life. When we have Jesus, we have his love that will, in turn, flow to others.

Open my heart today, Lord, to get at least a glimpse of your overwhelming love for me. I know it in my head and I'm asking you to reveal it to my heart.

DOING GOOD

Since future victory is sure, be strong and steady, always abounding in the Lord's work, for you know that nothing you do for the Lord is ever wasted as it would be if there were no resurrection.

1 CORINTHIANS 15:58 TLB

Living for the sake of others can be exhausting. Yet, that is exactly what the Lord called us to do. He wants us to serve others, love others, and lay our lives down for the sake of his glory. Despite our best intentions to live out that calling, we can still experience burn out—especially when it seems like day after day we are giving and not receiving anything in return. In our exhaustion we wonder if doing good for others is even worth the effort.

Jesus sees every selfless act. He notices you putting aside your own agenda for the sake of a friend. He sees you going without. He sees you striving to love beyond yourself and your own capabilities. Not only will he sustain your needs, he will bless you for your sacrifice. Doing good is usually not the easiest path, nor is it the most glamorous. But on that path you will meet your Savior, and he will be pleased with your efforts. The world may not acknowledge your good works, but Jesus will.

Jesus, sometimes it is a battle to do what is right, and to love others more than I love myself. Thank you for giving me the energy to persevere, and for filling me up when I feel tired and empty. Thank you for the life I find in you when I give my own up.

LIGHT IN THE DARKNESS

"I am the light of the world. Whoever follows me will not walk in darkness, but will have the light of life."

JOHN 8:12 ESV

When the world appears bleak and grey, when life seems too difficult to manage, and when our hope seems unreachable, we can be tempted to sink into despair. None of us are immune to depression. Depression can taunt even the most joyful of people. However if we aren't careful, it can settle over us like a heavy blanket. Depression is both lonely and scary. In that place, Jesus can feel far away, and doubts creep closer to our door.

Despite our disbelief and jaded faith, Jesus will still come and pick us up. He will open our tear-filled eyes to the blessings that surround us. We may feel hopeless, but he will fill our lives with joy again. Our faithful Father will call off the choking darkness and set us free from the hardships. All we have to do is focus on his goodness, call out to him, and wait. He will come and rescue us.

Jesus, thank you for your presence that is continuous light when darkness threatens to overtake me. You are my rescuer, my Savior, and the one who loves me perfectly through it all.

THE MOST INSPIRING

"Greater love has no one than this, that one lay down his life for his friends."

JOHN 15:13 NASB

It's not uncommon for us to be inspired by the people around us. Maybe someone's creativity inspired us to create. Maybe an appealing lifestyle drew us in. Maybe heroism challenged us. Or perhaps sacrificial love for others called us to compassion. Throughout the Bible are many inspirational people: David with his courage, Caleb with his commitment, Moses with his heroism, Paul with his passion, Daniel with his bravery, and Joseph with his leadership.

The most inspiring of all, though, is Jesus. He lived sacrificially, with open arms and a loving heart. He turned no one away and loved the unlovable. He walked on water, raised people from the dead, and healed the hurting. If all that wasn't enough, he did the unthinkable, willingly laying his life down for us. His life encompassed leadership, bravery, strength, heroism, and humility. If we modeled our lives after his, we would leave a lasting impact on many lives.

Jesus, you inspire me to live for others, to love others unconditionally, and to give grace abundantly. Thank you for your humble and gracious example. I long to be more like you.

NEED FOR FRIENDSHIP

He heals the brokenhearted
And binds up their wounds.
PSALM 147:3 NKJV

When God created us, he created a deep need for relationship. He intended for us to have family and friends. When that need isn't fulfilled, we feel terribly lonely and empty. Loneliness was not God's plan for any of us. And yet, we do have times in our lives where we feel intensely alone. We long for deep, authentic relationships. We desire to be surrounded by people we can share our lives with.

Our need for friends is universal. We all share the desire to love and be loved, to know and be known. But we can only be truly fulfilled by our relationship with Christ. He longs to have communion with us, just as much as we long to be heard, understood, and loved. He can heal the ache of loneliness with his presence.

Thank you, Jesus, that not only do you provide community, friends, and family, but you delight me with your presence. You are always there to love me, and spend my days with me.

NO CONDITIONS

Let us then with confidence draw near to the throne of grace, that we may receive mercy and find grace to help in time of need.

HEBREWS 4:16 ESV

It is hard to believe that love will remain forever. We assume that there are conditions put on love. *I will be loved if I am always good. I will be loved as long as I don't mess up. If I do x, y, and z, then I will always be loved.* The love the Father has for us comes without rules and regulations. There is absolutely nothing we can do or say that will take away his affection.

Despite our sin, we can confidently go to God for mercy, grace, and forgiveness, and he will welcome us. It's his unending love that gives us confidence to walk out our salvation with grace and boldness. We know that his love for us is limitless. It can't be earned or found. It is given as a gift that will not be taken back.

Thank you, Jesus, that I can have confidence that when I need you, when I need your grace, your mercy, and your unfailing love, you will not turn away from me. Thank you for the assurance that your love for me never wavers.

LOVED THROUGH LOSS

"So also you have sorrow now, but I will see you again, and your hearts will rejoice, and no one will take your joy from you."
JOHN 16:22 ESV

If you have ever lost something important to you, you know the feeling of intense pain and grief. It can be overwhelming—suffocating even. When we lose someone we love, whether that be a good friend, a child, or a family member, it can feel like we lost a part of ourselves. It is devastating. Especially if we feel alone in our grief.

When we experience loss, it feels like the pain of loss and separation will be a part of us forever and that we will never recover again. Grief is an intense and lonely place. As the world goes on, ours feels stuck in time. Loss is hard to overcome, and that ache seems as if it will become a permanent etch on our hearts. Even in the darkness, the loneliness, the confusion, he is there with you. He will always be our place of comfort if we allow him to be. He can dull that ache, heal the wounds that loss has created, and fill us again with hope, joy, and peace.

Jesus, thank you that even in this world though I may lose much, I will never lose you. Thank you that when I hurt, you hurt; when I cry, you cry. You love me through a loss so sweetly with your presence.

ABSOLUTE CERTAINTY

When I am afraid, I will put my confidence in you. Yes, I will trust the promises of God. And since I am trusting him, what can mere man do to me?

PSALM 56:3-4 TLB

Anytime we put our lives or hands in other people's care, it takes a great deal of trust. To trust someone is not always the easiest thing to do; yet, we do it daily when we step inside a car, ride a bus, or fly as a passenger on an airplane. Sometimes our lives are in a doctor's hands. Sometimes we put our hearts on the line when we choose to love someone. Trusting can involve a great deal of risk.

When we give our lives to God, we can trust that he will protect us. We can trust that his intentions toward us are always good. We can trust that he will never fail us. We can trust that he will give us love, peace, and the measure of grace we need. When we feel afraid, confused, and unsure, we can run to him and know that he will take care of us. When we trust in him, we are always in a safe place. Knowing that he will not let us down allows us to live a life free of fear.

Jesus, thank you for being my place of absolute certainty and trust. When I am afraid, I know that you will comfort all of my fears. While others may be difficult to trust, you are not.

A Beautiful Gift

No matter what happens, always be thankful, for this is God's will for you who belong to Christ Jesus.
1 THESSALONIANS 5:18 TLB

It is easy to be thankful when everything in life is going well. But it's a whole other story to be thankful when life is difficult. We always have a choice. We can be disgruntled with everything that is going wrong around us, allowing bitterness and discontentment to rob us of our joy and blessings. Or we can quiet our worried spirit, and choose gratitude.

Gratitude is a beautiful gift. It opens our eyes and hearts to all of the blessings that remain even in dire circumstances. Our bills may be mounting, but we can still be thankful for our healthy bodies. Our relationships may be hurting, but we can still be thankful to serve a God who heals and redeems. Our health may be failing, but we can still be thankful for God's unending mercy, compassion, and grace. We may feel overwhelmed and stressed, but we still have a God who is in control.

Thank you, Jesus, that gratitude is a gift. Help me count all the blessings around me. Thank you that even in times of trouble, my heart is still able to rejoice in your goodness.

HE IS STRONG

Surely God is my salvation;
I will trust and not be afraid.
The LORD, the LORD himself, is my strength and my defense;
he has become my salvation.

ISAIAH 12:2 NIV

So many times we tell ourselves, *I need to be strong. I am the rock of my family. I'm keeping it together at work. My friends rely on me to be there for them.* There's a burden to carry in so many areas of our lives, and sometimes we feel like we may just break under the weight.

But there's good news for us. Our strength doesn't need to come from our own power. God is happy to come alongside us and carry our burdens for us. There need be no fear of breaking because God is strong enough to manage it all. Indeed, you can operate in strength, but you are made stronger when you rely on the Lord to be your salvation.

Lord, thank you for carrying my heavy loads. I pray I would continue to trust you and look to you when I need help, rather than trying to push through on my own. Thank you for being my strength and defense in times of trouble.

SWEET RELIEF

When you pass through the waters, I will be with you;
and through the rivers, they shall not overwhelm you;
when you walk through fire you shall not be burned,
and the flame shall not consume you.

ISAIAH 43:2 ESV

There is nothing worse in life, than going through a hard time and feeling like you are all alone in it. Facing difficulties alone can be heart wrenching, confusing, and, well, lonely. If we are able to take a trusted friend into our hard times, the journey becomes easier. Having a support system, an ally, someone to whisper encouragement and love to our spirits, takes the edge off. It lightens our burdens.

Thankfully, it doesn't matter what we are enduring; we are never alone. Jesus is our faithful and trusted friend, and he is present. He is present in the good times and in the bad. Take a deep breath and know that even though this season in your life is difficult, you can lean into him and gather strength from his presence.

Jesus, your presence is such a sweet relief. Thank you that I don't have to journey alone; rather, I can always journey with you, my faithful and trusted friend.

A Clean Slate

O loving and kind God, have mercy. Have pity upon me and take away the awful stain of my transgressions. Oh, wash me, cleanse me from this guilt. Let me be pure again.

PSALM 51:1-2 TLB

Isn't it comforting to know that others aren't perfect? What's even better is that God loves us all anyway, regardless of how we may fail. We can be so hard on ourselves, expecting nothing less than a mistake-free existence. But when we have a remorseful heart, he forgives us and shows us mercy.

Just look at the prayer that King David wrote all those years ago. After making some of the biggest mistakes of his life, he knew that he could turn to his Father in heaven and have his slate wiped clean. We can do the same! Our incredible God shows us grace when we least deserve it, if we will only ask for it.

Lord, my life is full of mistakes. I'm asking for your forgiveness: for my sins to be washed away and my slate to be wiped clean. Show me mercy, Lord! Thank you for your compassion and your forgiving heart. I know I don't deserve it, but I will take this gift gladly.

LIST OF NEEDS

"Come to Me, all you who labor and are heavy laden, and I will give you rest. Take My yoke upon you and learn from Me, for I am gentle and lowly in heart, and you will find rest for your souls. For My yoke is easy and My burden is light."
MATTHEW 11:28-30 NKJV

If we sat down and wrote out a list of all the things we were worried about, chances are the list would be overwhelming. Finances. Relationships. Future plans. We can sit and stew in our worries until we lose our minds. But generally worry comes from a lack of trust or a fear of our needs not being met.

God promises to take care of us and of every single need that is listed on our hearts. We can trust him. Instead of wasting energy on the what-ifs, we can simply lay our needs at his feet and know that hasn't forgotten about us. In fact, he was aware of all of our worries before we even voiced them.

Jesus, I am so grateful that you are my provider. All of my needs will be met by you, so I don't need to worry.

FAITHFUL FRIEND

A real friend sticks closer than a brother.
PROVERBS 18:24 NLT

At the end of a long day, sometimes all we want is to sit with a good friend and talk—not for the purpose of speaking alone, but simply from a deep longing to be heard. We want to share our joys, our worries, our frustrations, and our hopes with someone who will listen. Who will focus on what we are saying. Someone who really cares. Everyone needs a friend like that.

It feels good to be heard. If we feel like we aren't, it is easy to fall into the trap of thinking we don't matter. We believe the lie that no one cares. God *does* care, and he *is* listening. When no one else is available, he is. He sees you. He wants to fill that lonely place inside you with his presence.

God, I am thankful that you are my faithful friend. You know me by name, and you are always willing to sit and listen to what is on my heart.

DESPERATE FOR A SAVIOR

We believe it is through the grace of our Lord Jesus that we
are saved.

ACTS 15:11 NIV

From the time we are little, we are conditioned to believe that if
we do good things, we will be rewarded with good things. Gold star
charts enforce it and soon turn into promotions and bonuses as we
reach adulthood. We become accustomed to this system and learn to
live by it.

It's not surprising, then, that many of us try to earn our salvation
by living a good life. Thankfully, that's not how God's grace works.
We are unable to achieve perfection. We constantly fall. Despite our
eager intentions, we make mistakes. We sin. We are desperate for
a Savior. Praise God that salvation is a gift freely given. We don't
deserve such beautiful grace, but he joyfully gives it to us.

Thank you, Jesus, that my salvation is a free gift. I am thankful
that I don't have to be perfect to have eternal life with you.

MET IN GRIEF

"Blessed are those who mourn,
for they will be comforted."
MATTHEW 5:4 NIV

To experience life fully, we need to be willing to feel deeply. We need to feel joy, peace, and love. And we need to feel loss and pain. Grief was never God's intention for us, but without it we wouldn't experience his goodness, comfort, and presence in the same measure. As we wrestle with grief, and the pain and confusion that accompany it, we can confidently know that we aren't in the struggle alone. Every sleepless night, every tear, every cry for help is heard.

As our faces are on the floor, he meets us with outstretched arms and a compassionate ear. He is our comforter when nothing else will do. He can ease the hurt that crushes our hearts when we press into him.

Jesus, thank you that in every path I take, even in a path of loss, you are always there with me. You don't leave me in my grief to fend for myself; you meet me there in it.

TEMPORARY STRUGGLES

"God blesses you who are hungry now,
for you will be satisfied.
God blesses you who weep now,
for in due time you will laugh."

LUKE 6:21 NLT

Sometimes it seems as if life will never get easier. We wake up with the same struggles and trials day after day. Trials that we grow weary of battling. We wonder when we will find rest and relief. In our suffering it can be difficult to see God's goodness, and we feel as if we will never experience joy or happiness again.

God promises that our trials and struggles are only temporary. He assures us that he will replace our aches and pains with happiness and laughter. It's in that promise that we can find comfort.

Jesus, I am thankful that my struggles are only temporary. I am thankful that you promise to lift my pain and fill my heart with joy and peace. Thank you for comforting me when I need your presence.

JESUS WILL NEVER LEAVE YOU

The LORD himself goes before you and will be with you; he will never leave you nor forsake you. Do not be afraid; do not be discouraged.

DEUTERONOMY 31:8 NIV

When darkness and heaviness surrounds us, it can feel like we can't breathe. Depression can slowly sneak up on us like a thief in the night, or it can crash down on us suddenly. Regardless of how it descends on us, it can be a scary thing to fight off.

There is always help in our place of utter hopelessness. Jesus is the light that pierces even the darkest corners of our heart. In hard times, we can call out to him. He promises peace and help. He will lift the sadness and cover us with joy that can only come from him. Depression can threaten to steal our life, but Jesus gives it right back. He saves us. He protects us. Set your eyes on him and take a big deep breath. He has you.

Lord, I need your light in my life. When things get too hard, please come and take me out of the darkness. Thank you that you gave me a life full of hope and peace.

THE GATEWAY TO LIFE

"Very truly I tell you, unless a kernel of wheat falls to the
ground and dies, it remains only a single seed. But if it dies, it
produces many seeds."
JOHN 12:24 NIV

Fall in the northern states is spectacular. The intense colors and the
crisp, cool air is a reminder that winter is on its way. The dying leaves
waft beautifully to the ground in gentle submission to their maker's
plan. It's a time of death. Jesus spoke of this principle in John 12
when he said there must be death in order for life to come forth. Paul
testified in Galatians 2 that he had been crucified with Christ and was
now dead to self, sin, and the world. He no longer lived—Christ lived in
and through him. The power of sin was gone and new life was born.

Are you hanging onto something this morning that Christ is
asking you to bring to the cross? Sin and willfulness must die for
resurrection to occur. Death is the gateway to life.

Thank you, Jesus, for loving me enough to die for me and
then inviting me to share in that death. In that place, new life
begins. I choose to lay down my own agenda at the foot of
the cross this morning. Thank you for raising me to newness of
life!

OCTOBER

"For I know the plans
I have for you," says the L<small>ORD</small>.
"They are plans for good and
not for disaster,
to give you a future and a hope."

JEREMIAH 29:11 NLT

COURAGE BEYOND CAPACITY

Wait for the LORD;
be strong, and let your heart take courage;
wait for the LORD!
    PSALM 27:14 NRSV

When we feel like we can't possibly take one more step, or summon up any more courage. When our struggles deplete us of every last bit of strength. When we throw in the towel, call it quits, and say we can't...

It is the Lord that bends down before us, and whispers in our ear, "Beloved, yes you can. You can because I will equip you. You can because in your weakness, I am there. Because your courage is from me, and of me. Because I am faithful. Because your story is being written, and it is a story of courage and bravery beyond human capacity. Because I love you. Because I am with you. Because I will never leave you."

Thank you, Jesus, for being the author of my life. Thank you that you give me courage beyond my own capability and understanding. Teach me how to lean on you all of the days of my life.

NEVER HOPELESS

If we hope for what we do not see, we wait for it with patience.

ROMANS 8:25 ESV

Have you ever looked at a situation, sighed, and declared, "Oh, it's hopeless"? Even in the most dire of circumstances there is hope to be found. Sometimes we have to wait patiently for a better outcome, and that can be extremely difficult.

In waiting, we can either turn to discouragement and disbelief, or we can kneel and pray, putting our faith in God's goodness that stirs up hope. Hope is looking beyond our narrow perspective and limited view. It is the faith we put in the tiny details that we can't see but ultimately make up the bigger and more glorious picture. Hope is the confidence in knowing that no matter what happens, we will not be broken, and we will not be alone. Hope is that complete confidence that God's intentions toward us are good, and that his mighty hand will save us from destruction.

Jesus, I am so grateful that no matter what "hopeless" situation I find myself in, you give me hope and a sense of peace in the midst of chaos.

I Am Enough

Before I formed you in the womb I knew you,
before you were born I set you apart;
I appointed you as a prophet to the nations.

JEREMIAH 1:5 NIV

In the back of every woman's mind there is that unrelenting question that pierces the most hidden place of the heart and has the ability to crush with the dreaded answer. *Am I enough?* As a child? As a parent? As a sibling? As a friend? As a professional?

Our failures, inadequacies, and imperfections tell us we are not enough. They say we aren't worthy. That there are others out there who are more capable and more qualified. It's such a heart-wrenching lie. We are enough simply because God says we are. He created us perfectly in his image. We can stand confident, knowing that whatever role we are in we are enough to fill it. We are enough and we are dearly and passionately loved. So, shake off all your insecurities and embrace the identity Jesus has given you.

Jesus, when I feel small and inadequate, fill my heart with the knowledge that you declare that I am enough. I am worthy and I am loved. I am yours. You equip me. Thank you that you call me to do things in your strength that I never thought possible.

LIFE-GIVING JOY

In the day of trouble he will keep me safe in his dwelling;
he will hide me in the shelter of his sacred tent
and set me high upon a rock.
Then my head will be exalted
above the enemies who surround me;
at his sacred tent I will sacrifice with shouts of joy;
I will sing and make music to the LORD.
Hear my voice when I call, LORD;
be merciful to me and answer me.

   PSALM 27:5-7 NIV

Have you ever encountered someone and wondered how in the world
they were so joyful? Maybe they were terminally ill, or living in extreme
poverty, or perhaps they didn't seem to have a friend in the world. You
can't help but feel compassion for their situation, and yet they remain
content—joy oozes out of their pores. It is perplexing and intriguing.

Joy is not circumstantial. It differs from happiness that comes and
goes depending on the day. Joy is rooted deep inside every believer
with the ability to grow and flourish. It is not something we can
muster up ourselves; rather, it is a gift from God that comes only
from knowing and loving him. We can choose to live with deep joy
regardless of what is happening around us. In that joy, our lives
glorify God, and attract others to him. Joy is life giving: a weapon
against depression and darkness. And it is extremely contagious. Take
hold of it and declare it yours today.

Jesus, when times are hard, help me to choose joy again
and again. Let the joy that you give me be a witness and a
testimony to the love you have for me.

LOVE COMPLETELY

Above all, love each other deeply, because love covers over a multitude of sins.
1 PETER 4:8 NIV

Love is one of those things that we just can't measure. We either love or we don't. We can't choose to love those around us just a little. We are either all-in, all-given, all-committed, and all-purposed, or we aren't.

Loving can be messy, difficult, and even painful. Sometimes we can feel completely emptied out and dried up. Loving is laying our lives, our hearts, and our own desires down for the sake of others. We love, knowing there is a risk of being rejected. Of being hurt and disappointed. Of feeling battered and bruised. But we love completely because that is the only way to love—the way that Jesus loves us.

Jesus, continue to teach me how to love entirely without hesitation. Thank you for being the measure of love in my life. Help me to love others the way you do: fiercely and passionately.

INSATIABLE MONSTER

Don't love money; be satisfied with what you have. For God
has said,
"I will never fail you.
I will never abandon you."
HEBREWS 13:5 NLT

Discontentment can be an irrational and insatiable monster to feed.
And yet, sometimes it makes its home in the very pit of our stomachs.
Our eyes can be quick to remind us of what we don't have and our
hearts quick to declare we don't have enough.

The easiest way to rid ourselves from that greedy monster is to simply
stop feeding it. Instead of looking at what we don't have, we say
a quick prayer of gratitude for what we do have. Eventually that
want for more will evaporate. We need to make a direct choice to be
content with the body, job, home, and family God has given us. The
more we speak thanksgiving, the lighter our hearts get and the less
they wander. Contentment brings peace, and it allows us to inhale all
the unseen and unspoken blessings in our lives.

Thank you, Jesus, that you have given me such a beautiful life.
Thank you for your salvation and for your unending peace.
Thank you that you are truly all I need in this life.

THE BURDEN OF WORRY

I asked the LORD for help, and he answered me.
He saved me from all that I feared.
Those who go to him for help are happy,
and they are never disgraced.

PSALM 34:4-5 NCV

There is much in the day-to-day to be anxious about if we let
our hearts stray in that direction. We live in a world filled with
heartache, violence, pain, uncertainty and turmoil. We can quickly be
bogged down in worry. Everyday concerns like bills, work decisions,
relationship issues, and future decisions crowd our minds. Put
together, it can be overwhelming. How can we possibly have a spirit
at ease?

In these times, the Lord wants us to trust in him. By trusting, we can
take the burdens of worry off our shoulders where they don't belong.
Rather than taking ownership and responsibility of the world's
problems, God wants us to lay them at his feet. We let go, release
the anxiety that threatens to overtake us, and let him fill us with his
peace.

Jesus, thank you that you ask me to come and lay my burdens
of worry at your feet. Thank you for your incredible peace that
lives in me.

LEARNED THANKFULNESS

Every good and perfect gift is from above, coming down from the Father of the heavenly lights, who does not change like shifting shadows.

JAMES 1:17 NIV

Thankfulness is something that needs to be learned, and then practiced daily. It doesn't come easy for most of us. Often we choose to focus on things in life that aren't going well. A grumbling spirit comes more naturally than a thankful one. But it steals our joy and weighs us down.

When we start to practice thankfulness, our eyes open up to all of the blessings that surround us. Before we know it, our list of complaints diminishes, and a much longer list of gratitude grows. Our hearts become lighter, and we see all the wonderful ways that the Lord provides and cares for us.

Thank you, Lord, that you are a gift giver and you love to surprise me daily. Open my eyes to your goodness, and create in me a thankful heart.

OUR EXAMPLE OF COMPASSION

He takes care of people like a shepherd.
He gathers them like lambs in his arms
and carries them close to him.
ISAIAH 40:11 NCV

What causes our hearts to stir? Do we weep with those who weep?
Can we feel others' pain? Are we moved to serve? Or are we so caught
up in our lives that we fail to see the needs around us.

Compassion is powerful; it calls us to action. It leads us to hurt with
the hurt, to give to those who need, to love the unloved. Without
compassion, our hearts grow steely and hard. We lose the ability to
see people how God sees them. If we lack compassion, it could be a
sign that we are in desperate need of God in our lives. Jesus is moved
to help when he sees you hurting, and he rushes in to save. He is the
definition of compassion: our example.

Thank you, Jesus, that you make every day a new day. Thank
you that you show me compassion and love. Your compassion
moves me to be gracious and tenderhearted toward others.

PRAISE ALWAYS

Let everything alive give praises to the Lord!
You praise him!
Hallelujah!

PSALM 150:6 TLB

We can praise God and weep at the same time. It sounds impossible, but with God it is not. Our hearts can feel heavy; yet, we can still praise God in our trials because he is good. He is good when things are hard. He is good when the future seems bleak. He is good when the rest of the world isn't. He is good all the time.

Sometimes praising God when it's the last thing we want to do, is actually the best thing we can do. When we praise God, we draw nearer to him. We can praise God with our actions, with our voices, and with our attitudes. Our praise confirms in our spirits that he is worthy, that he is holy, and that he is sovereign. Praising him declares that he is the center of our lives, and that he has overcome every struggle we face.

Jesus, may I always glorify and praise you regardless of how my days are going. May my reaction to hard times be to speak of your goodness and your faithfulness. Let me never forget how worthy you are.

THE LORD'S DELIGHT

The LORD takes pleasure in his people;
he adorns the humble with victory.

PSALM 149:4 NRSV

A parent's love for a child is so tender. New parents can't help but delight themselves in their child. They are overjoyed with every single detail. They can't get enough of the holding, hugging, and kissing. Their eyes light up with excitement when they talk about their brand new baby. They speak good things over the child and hope for the very best. They concern themselves with every need the child has: big or small.

That is how the Lord feels about you—his child. He loves everything about you; he loves to spend time with you and meet your every need. He will go to the ends of the earth to protect you. He even laid his life down for yours. He is your loving and faithful Father who delights in your very existence.

God, your love for me is so tender. I am amazed that you feel such tremendous joy when you gaze at me. I am not worthy of the love you give me so freely, but I thank you for it.

PROMISES FULFILLED

This is what the LORD says:
"I will go before you, Cyrus,
and level the mountains.
I will smash down gates of bronze
and cut through bars of iron.
And I will give you treasures hidden in the darkness—
secret riches.
I will do this so you may know that I am the LORD,
the God of Israel, the one who calls you by name."
        ISAIAH 45:2-3 NLT

The world is quick to offer us promises of wealth, health, prosperity, and peace. But those promises lack follow through and leave disappointment in their wake. There is only one who can offer promises of complete peace.

It is in our hopelessness that we cling to the promises of God. It is in that place of utter discouragement that our hunger for faith is born. And the Lord diligently feeds our faith with his promises. Weaved throughout Scripture are his promises to protect us, love us endlessly, and fill us with an unshakeable peace. We can hope for the impossible, dream of the unattainable, and see light in utter darkness because of the promises God breathes into our very existence.

My hope is in your fulfilled promises, God. Thank you that your promises give me strength and courage in every situation.

VICTORY OVER SIN

No temptation has overtaken you that is not common to man.
God is faithful, and he will not let you be tempted beyond
your ability, but with the temptation he will also provide the
way of escape, that you may be able to endure it.

1 CORINTHIANS 10:13 ESV

In our walk with God sometimes it can feel like we are continually
hitting roadblocks. We sin, repent, pick ourselves up, and then fall
again. Despite our genuine heart's desire to choose what is right and
to live victoriously over sin, we feel trapped and enslaved to our old
sin patterns.

Maybe it is anger that causes you to stumble, or dishonesty, or
unkindness. You go to bed at night feeling defeated and discouraged.
Maybe you wonder what is wrong with you and why you can't seem
to get your act together despite your best intentions. When you
fail, the Lord wants you to raise your eyes to the sky. Jesus gave you
victory over those sins when he was nailed to the cross. Every day is a
brand new day. That is his gift to you. Embrace it fully.

Jesus, thank you for your work on the cross. Thank you that
you see my struggles, you see my failures, and yet you call me
victorious. Thank you for giving me the courage to see every
day as a brand new day.

WASTED WORRY

Therefore do not be anxious, saying, 'What shall we eat?' or 'What shall we drink?' or 'What shall we wear?' For the Gentiles seek after all these things, and your heavenly Father knows that you need them all. But seek first the kingdom of God and his righteousness, and all these things will be added to you.
MATTHEW 6:31-33 ESV

Many of us lay awake at night worrying about finances. How are we going to make the paycheck stretch all month, pay for that unexpected expense, or dig ourselves out of debt that seems to be increasing? We exhaust ourselves worrying about money, our homes, and our health. We strive to maintain financial success, often working ourselves ragged and sick.

Our worry is pointless. We can work hard and should be wise with our resources, but it is ultimately God that we have to thank for our provision. He sees our needs, and he will meet them. If we rely on ourselves to provide for our every need, we prohibit God from showing up in our lives in big ways. Only God can provide exactly what we need.

Jesus, help me to keep my eyes and heart centered on you. Help me to strive for more of you and less of what the world has to offer.

WHAT NEXT?

Show me the right path, O Lord;
point out the road for me to follow.
Lead me by your truth and teach me,
for you are the God who saves me.
All day long I put my hope in you.

PSALM 25:4-5 NLT

What's next? That's always the question isn't it? It doesn't matter what stage in life we reach, we are always looking for the next step to take. But our paths aren't always so clear. Sometimes the next step seems foggy. It's hard to decipher what God's will is. Should we further our education? In what field? Should we get married? Go on that mission trip? They are all good questions that don't always have clear answers.

When we are grappling with life's biggest decisions, there is wisdom and direction to be found that reaches beyond counselors, self-help books, and well-intentioned friends. Seek Jesus out during these times. Read his Word; ask him to match your heart with his. Let him guide your steps. He will fill you with unimaginable peace as you make that next big move.

Jesus, direct my steps in the big decisions and in the small. I know for certain that as long as I let you lead me, I will be in the center of your will.

THE INSPIRING WORD

All Scripture is inspired by God and is useful for teaching, for showing people what is wrong in their lives, for correcting faults, and for teaching how to live right.

2 TIMOTHY 3:16 NCV

Does your Bible sit on your nightstand untouched and dusty? Sometimes we think of Scripture as outdated, boring, and tiring. In our culture's undeniable pursuit for quick answers and instant entertainment, God's Word can get lost. We get caught up in the busyness and try to live without it.

But, oh, how we need his Word to direct us. It is the roadmap toward knowing his heart and being more like him. To know God is to know his Word. Carving out time to read and soak in his Word is worth our every effort. In it we find his teaching, hope, grace, and love. Picking up the Bible will strengthen our hearts. It will give us renewed inspiration to follow him, obey him, and dedicate our lives to him. Without it, life is muddled and hopeless.

Jesus, thank you for your Word that not only guides me but inspires me to live for you. It is a precious gift! Help me to hide it in the deepest corners of my heart. Thank you that it breathes life and hope into my spirit.

THE LAST LEG

Let us not become weary in doing good, for at the proper time we will reap a harvest if we do not give up.

GALATIANS 6:9 NIV

The last leg of the race is usually the hardest. Runners are exhausted. In that state, they can forget what their purpose was in the first place. What is the point of working so hard, denying themselves comfort and rest? The end seems so far away, and the prize unattainable. They are tempted to give up. Their minds tell them to keep going, but their muscles scream in protest.

Following God isn't always the easiest path. In fact, he warns us that the road will be difficult. But persevering to live for him and him alone is worth every last ounce of our energy. The world will be quick to tell us that it's not worth it, but Jesus says to carry on. Be strong. Be steadfast. Keep going. Don't give up. God is our biggest cheerleader. Despite your weariness, despite the roadblocks, the pain, and the heartache, know that the end is near and it is more than you could ever imagine.

God, when I am tempted to give up, please give me the strength to keep going. Please take my weariness and replace it with a determination that only comes from you.

LIKE NONE OTHER

He will not let your foot be moved;
he who keeps you will not slumber.

PSALM 121:3 ESV

Who can we trust? We desire to put our faith in the people around us, but it's disheartening because many of those we put our trust in fail us. We can trust God. He is like none other. We can look to him, lean on him, and know that we will not fall because he is faithful. When everyone else's word is weightless and shaky, his is strong and constant. When people fail to show up, he is there. When we suffer disappointment and betrayal, he heals our wounds. He is our protector and constant advocate.

God does not ignore our cries for help or our pleas for mercy. He is there at our side when every tear drops. We can be confident that he will never abandon us. He is reliable, and dependable. His love for, and commitment to, us is never changing. We can trust him completely and freely. He will not disappoint.

Jesus, in a world that makes it hard to trust and depend on others, thank you that I can always count on your constant presence in my life. Thank you that I can trust you completely.

CREATED FOR A PURPOSE

We know that in all things God works for the good of those who love him, who have been called according to his purpose.

ROMANS 8:28 NIV

A life without purpose can feel hopeless—mundane at best. Without a specific goal or direction, it is easy to question ourselves. Why do I get up in the morning? Why am I working so hard? Does my life have significance or meaning? Am I making an impact on the world? The questions will be unending because we were created for a purpose. We weren't created to float mindlessly throughout our days. When we live that way, we feel a deep sense of emptiness and loneliness.

We were created first to love God. It's in our love for him that will find our reason for living. In loving him our lives are transformed. The more we fix our eyes on him, the more we desire to reflect him. The more we reflect him, the less empty we feel. Worldly possessions lose their luster, selfishness diminishes, and we find fulfillment, contentment, and *purpose* in living for him.

Jesus, when I feel lost, let me find fulfillment and purpose in simply loving and serving you. May my contentment in life come from knowing you. Draw me close to you.

FREE TO LIVE

For freedom Christ has set us free; stand firm therefore, and do not submit again to a yoke of slavery.
GALATIANS 5:1 ESV

Despite being handed our freedom, we sometimes slide back into the habit of living as if we are prisoners. We allow what used to enslave our hearts to continue to lead us down dangerous paths. We forget that we have complete freedom from old thought patterns and sin cycles. Then we beat ourselves up in frustration, wondering why we just can't seem to get it right. We desire to live a life of freedom, yet can't fully grasp the gift of grace and forgiveness.

We have the power to shake off the condemnation and shame that haunt us. When Jesus died on the cross, he gave us a new life. He took all our shame on himself and declared us forgiven and free. We can stand strong, knowing that we belong to Jesus. Sin doesn't own us. Our pasts no longer define us. We were made brand new without any chains. Confidently accept the love and grace he gives you today.

Jesus, thank you for giving me a brand new life in you. Thank you for freeing me from shame and condemnation and allowing me to live full of grace.

THE YES TO

The yes to all of God's promises is in Christ, and through Christ
we say yes to the glory of God.

2 CORINTHIANS 1:20 NCV

We all go through seasons in life when we doubt if God is really good
to us. But tasting the goodness of God is often as simple as opening
our hearts to receive what he has promised through Christ.

We may feel unworthy or even unready, but if we have said yes to
salvation, then we have also said yes to God's promises, his goodness,
and his eternal glory.

God, I say yes, right now, to your promises for my life. I say
yes to your glory, your goodness, and your grace. I thank you
that your salvation and your promises are mine in Christ Jesus.
I ask you for the strength to continue to say yes even when I
feel ineligible. I know that in Christ I am a new creation who is
worthy of goodness.

MAKE A CHANGE

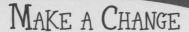

Do not conform to the pattern of this world, but be transformed by the renewing of your mind. Then you will be able to test and approve what God's will is—his good, pleasing and perfect will.

ROMANS 12:2 NIV

We want change, but we struggle to get or stay on task with our goals. "One day, I'll..." is the enemy of "Today, I am...", yet it seems that as long as change hurts more than staying the same, we vacillate between our desires and our comfort.

It is often so with surrendering to the Holy Spirit. He longs to do "greater things than these," and while this appeals to us, the comfort of doing nothing seems reassuring, safe, and predictable. We find, at last, that the center of God's will truly is the safest place for our lives. Knowing that, we revel in him as he molds and inspires us. We were created to do good things.

Thank you, Father, for the changes you are making in my life. I enjoy being transformed by you, polished like the silver brought out for special occasions. You are good to me. Let your word do the work in my life that you would like.

HE CARES ABOUT YOU, UNIQUELY

Just as each of us has one body with many members, and these members do not all have the same function, so in Christ we, though many, form one body, and each member belongs to all the others.
ROMANS 12:4-5 NIV

Each of us has a function. We don't operate like one another because we aren't fashioned that way. We often don't agree upon priorities—beyond dwelling in Christ and living in love—because we are each made to carry different aspects of God's glory.

So often, we read this verse as an adjuration to play nicely with people of other denominations. That's not it, though. It's a glorification of our wondrously creative God, and an encouragement to each take up our gifts, allowing others to do the same. Our gifts are just as personal as our salvation experiences. When we finally embrace our interdependence, we honor each other and operate in unity. We embrace who we are in Christ and let go of what we are not. To have the liberty to do so is an aspect of what it is to be truly free in Christ, and to operate in freedom.

Father, thank you for the intricate care you used in making me. Help me to recognize what gifts within me are actually not universal values for everyone else, but are your unique signature of grace upon my life. I love you! Thank you for making me so thoughtfully, and letting me discover your hand on me. Your gifts are always good. Please show me how to foster what gifts you reveal throughout my day, today.

WEIGHT OF WORRY

Anxiety in a man's heart weighs him down,
but a good word makes him glad.
PROVERBS 12:25 ESV

Worry fills our head with questions that may never have answers and possibilities that may never come to pass. We become wearied as even our momentary troubles outweigh our peace. It is in these times that the encouraging words of a friend can become the catalyst to change our uncertainty into strength and our doubt into restored faith.

By surrounding ourselves with the type of people who regularly speak the truth, we unknowingly secure our own peace and future gladness.

God, when I begin to feel anxious, I pray that you would bring a friend to speak your truth to me. Help me also to be an encouraging friend who brings peace to those around me.

COMPASSION THAT NEVER CEASES

The steadfast love of the LORD never ceases,
his mercies never come to an end;
they are new every morning;
great is your faithfulness.

LAMENTATIONS 3:22-23 NRSV

Has anyone shown you compassion when you needed it? The answer is yes for all of mankind. God is a compassionate God, and his compassions will never fail. You might have been failed by others many times, but you will not be failed by God. Not only will his compassion not fail, it is regenerated *every single morning*. Fresh compassion pours over your life and your circumstances each day.

Compassion says, "I understand what you are going through. I know this is hard." It doesn't point from a distance and ridicule you for not being tough enough. No, compassion—rather, God himself—comes alongside you in your suffering with a promise that he will not leave or forsake you in your hour of need.

Father, thank you that when I am at my weakest, you are there. You have compassion toward me. Thank you for your steady, kind love today.

GOOD AND PERFECT

Whatever is good and perfect is a gift coming down to us from God our Father, who created all the lights in the heavens. He never changes or casts a shifting shadow.

JAMES 1:17 NLT

Take the next few minutes to pause and consider all the good, all the beauty in your life. You may be in a season that makes this easy, or perhaps now is a time that doesn't feel particularly "good and perfect."

Peonies in June, the wink of a quarter moon, loving and being loved, these are gifts from God. Your Father is a good father, a giver of good gifts. This doesn't change, even when your circumstances do.

Lord, every day you send gifts, reminding me you are good and I am yours. Help me see your gifts even through tears. You are constant; you are perfect. Thank you for loving me.

TRULY AWESOME

The heavens declare the glory of God;
the skies proclaim the work of his hands.
Day after day they pour forth speech;
night after night they reveal knowledge.

PSALM 19:1-2 NIV

Amazing beauty is all around us, so much so that we can become
used to it. When was the last time you stopped to marvel at God's
incredible creativity?

Study a flower. Read about the human eye. Watch the sun rise or
set. Write down your dreams. Spend some time just soaking in the
awesomeness of the creator.

God, you are truly awesome. Every time I look at the sky, I see
something new. Even a few attentive minutes on this earth
reveal miracle and majesty everywhere I look. How beautiful
you have made this world, and how blessed I am to live in it.

NO DARKNESS

This is the message we have heard from him and declare to you: God is light; in him there is no darkness at all.

1 JOHN 1:5 NIV

In total darkness, we instinctively seek light. We turn on our phones, fumble for a light switch, light a candle. With a single light source, the darkness can be overcome. We can find our way.

This same principle applies to our hearts. God is pure light, and with him, we can overcome any darkness we face. No temptation, no addiction, no sin is too powerful for God to conquer.

Father, I know that whenever and wherever I face darkness, I need only seek your face. You are all good, all pure, all light. I surrender my struggle with the darkness to you, and ask you to help me overcome it. I want to live in your pure light.

JUST SAY NO

Submit yourselves, then, to God.
Resist the devil, and he will flee from you.
JAMES 4:7 NIV

Submit to God; resist the devil. It seems simple, so why do culture—and our own lives—so often say the opposite? How often do we give in to temptation and resist the one leading us to our best life?

Until we surrender our lives to the one who wants only good for us, only peace and light, we are subject to the one who wants to destroy us. He will leave, running scared, but not until we stand with God and tell him "no."

Lord, I come before you today filled with regret for the many times I've chosen dark over light, what is easy over what is right. I want to submit my life to you, but I need your help. Strengthen me, Lord, and help me send the enemy running.

REAL LOVE

Since ancient times no one has heard,
no ear has perceived,
no eye has seen any God besides you,
who acts on behalf of those who wait for him.
    ISAIAH 64:4 NIV

Authenticity. It matters, doesn't it? We wonder if the gem, the handbag, the promise, is real. We've heard the expression, "If it sounds too good to be true, it probably is," so we scrutinize the people and possessions in our lives, looking for authenticity.

What great comfort we can take in our God: the one, true God! All his promises are true; all his gifts are good. His love is authentic, and it is ours to claim.

Lord, you are God. The one, the only, the Almighty God. Who am I that you should act on my behalf, that you should speak into my life? And yet you do. May my love for you be authentic and my words of praise be true.

SING!

Sing praises to God, sing praises!
Sing praises to our King, sing praises!
For God is the King of all the earth;
Sing praises with understanding.
    PSALM 47:6-7 NKJV

We may not all have the voice of an angel, but we can all sing, no matter how good or bad it sounds to us. God created you with a voice and with lips that can praise him for all the good things he has done. He is the king of the earth and the king of our hearts. He will delight in your song of praise, even if he is the only one that appreciates it!

So, sing praises to God. Sing, because you understand his goodness. Sing, because you understand his grace. Sing, because he is worthy!

God, you are the king of all the earth. You have been good to me. You have shown your grace toward me. Teach me to delight in singing your praises. I know you delight in me when I praise you.

NOVEMBER

Everything God created is good,
and nothing is to be rejected if it is
received with thanksgiving.

1 TIMOTHY 4:4

THE STRUGGLE WILL END

Let your roots grow down into him, and let your lives be built on him. Then your faith will grow strong in the truth you were taught, and you will overflow with thankfulness.

COLOSSIANS 2:7 NLT

In the weeks leading up to Thanksgiving, the theme of gratitude becomes all but inescapable. This can be wonderful, reminding us of all the good in our lives, but it can also be painful. What if we're in a season where thankfulness eludes us? What if counting our blessings takes no time at all?

If this is you, you are not alone. There will always be times when struggle seems more prevalent than blessing, when gratitude seems like an impossible requirement, and faith, once so familiar, has gone into hiding. Release your heart from any guilt bubbling up inside, and sink your roots into Jesus. Pore over his Word, and let his love and truth pour over you. The struggle will end. The blessings will come. All will be well.

Lord, today I lift up those whose hearts are breaking, and those whose hearts are full. May gratitude and faith overflow from one into the other, and may all our roots intertwine in the rich, fertile soil of your love and truth.

CONTINUE IN CHRIST

Just as you received Christ Jesus as Lord,
continue to live your lives in him.

COLOSSIANS 2:6 NIV

Receiving Christ causes a wonderful transformation. But there is fullness to the Christian life that goes beyond salvation. The Scripture says that we *continue* our lives in him. This means that every day we have the opportunity to grow in our relationship with God.

As we develop our relationship with Christ, we experience a deep assurance of our faith and we are empowered to live a full life. It is easy to be thankful for all of the good things Jesus is doing in your life as you go from strength to strength.

Lord Jesus, thank you for what I have been learning through your holy Scriptures. Remind me to continue in my faith by following your example and listening to your voice. I am so thankful for my salvation and I am even more thankful that you choose to be in relationship with me.

SATISFIED

Because your love is better than life,
my lips will glorify you.
I will praise you as long as I live,
and in your name I will lift up my hands.
I will be fully satisfied as with the richest of foods;
with singing lips my mouth will praise you.

PSALM 63:3-5 NIV

There are times in our lives when we really need answers or a breakthrough, and sometimes we just want to be blessed. Our loving Father says to simply ask.

God wants to give us good gifts. You might not want to ask for things because you feel they are too much, or too specific. But God is able to handle our requests—he won't give us things that will bring us harm or that we will use for our selfish gain. He knows what is best for us. His love is better than life itself, and he knows exactly how to satisfy us.

Lord, there are many things that I need and many things I want. I ask you for them now because I know that you are a loving Father who wants to answer me today.

CHASED BY GRACE

Surely goodness and mercy shall follow me
All the days of my life;
And I will dwell in the house of the LORD
Forever.
  PSALM 23:6 NKJV

We leave footprints as we walk along the journey of life. Some of these footprints are left from walking in the dirt and they need to be cleaned up because they don't belong to the path of righteousness.

God wants to lead you in the right direction. As you live in his ways your path will be followed by goodness, and his mercy will clean up those footsteps that have gone in the wrong direction. His grace will follow you all of your life. It is by this grace that you will dwell in the house of the Lord forever!

Heavenly Father, I want to dwell in your house forever. I trust in your goodness and mercy to follow me as I journey through life with you before me, behind me, and beside me. Allow me to know your presence today.

PROVISION FOR THE GENEROUS

May He who supplies seed to the sower, and bread for food, supply and multiply the seed you have sown and increase the fruits of your righteousness.

2 CORINTHIANS 9:10 NKJV

The beginning of generosity is provision. Just as a farmer requires seed for a harvest, we must also be provided with something to sow. God has supplied you with everything you need to help in growing his kingdom. He will increase your resources as you diligently plant the seeds of faith.

As God multiplies your resources, he will also increase the harvest, that is, the good that comes from what you have sown. He gives to you generously that you might be generous. Be encouraged to give from what he has given you, and watch the blessings in your life increase.

Heavenly Father, you continue to supply me with all that I need. Help me to sow my seeds of faith so that I might see growth in my life and in the lives of others. Lead me to generosity so that your work will be done on earth as it is in heaven.

HE REJOICES OVER YOU

The LORD your God in your midst,
The Mighty One, will save;
He will rejoice over you with gladness.
ZEPHANIAH 3:17 NKJV

Parents are usually insanely proud of their children. It doesn't seem to matter what particular gift a child might have, a parent will always find something in that child to praise. A parent's love is not about what the child can do, but about who they are. They see a beautiful heart and amazing potential.

Our heavenly Father feels like this about us—only much more. Not only is he always present, he's protective, proud, and loving. Can you imagine him today, being so happy to be near you that he sings and rejoices over you! You are his daughter, and you are loved.

Father, sometimes I forget that you love me for who I am, not what I do. You see my heart and you rejoice over me. Give me the confidence to walk through life with the knowledge that I have a heavenly Father who delights in me so much that he can't help but sing!

THE MANY WONDERS OF GOD

Many, O LORD my God,
are the wonders you have done.
The things you planned for us.
None can compare with you;
were I to speak and tell of your deeds,
they would be too many to declare.

PSALM 40:5 NIV

It is good to give God the glory for all the things that are too
wonderful for words. We know from the Bible that God has acted
powerfully on many occasions to preserve his chosen people. We
know that Jesus performed spectacular miracles. The Holy Spirit
moved mightily on the early church and still shows his power today.

God didn't stop at making the earth; he continues to make wonderful
things in this life. You can probably think of many examples of how
God has done great things for you. Imagine how many believers can
tell these stories as well... there are too many to declare!

Lord God, I thank you for all the wonderful plans you have
in store for my life. You are too great for words, and I simply
declare that you are awesome!

RADIANT REFLECTION

He is the radiance of the glory of God and the exact imprint of his nature, and he upholds the universe by the word of his power. After making purification for sins, he sat down at the right hand of the Majesty on high.

HEBREWS 1:3 ESV

Jesus was no ordinary man. We know this of course, but do we acknowledge Jesus as the divine being who had equality with God? When Jesus came to earth, he revealed God's nature to us. Because he is the radiance of God, he reflects a God that is both powerful and loving.

Though Jesus was divine, he came to earth as a man so that he could carry out the will of God. This was to be the ultimate sacrifice for all of humanity, so that our sins would be covered. Jesus, now seated with God in heaven, came for you. He upholds the universe, and he upholds *you* with his Word.

Jesus, I thank you that you humbled yourself as a man so that I might come to know the fullness of God through you. I worship you today because you have revealed yourself as a holy and loving God.

CONTINUAL PRAISE

From the rising of the sun to its going down
The LORD's name is to be praised.

PSALM 113:3 NKJV

What would it look like to be a woman who praises God from the time she awakens each morning until the time she falls asleep each night? Not only would we be pleasing God as we worship him constantly, but we would also effect an incredible change in our personal outlook.

Intentional, continual praise can only naturally result in intentional, continual joy. When I choose to look at each moment as a moment in which to be thankful and worshipful, then I will find in each moment beauty, joy, and satisfaction.

Lord, I praise you for your love for me. I pray that you would help me to be a woman who praises you all day, every day. I pray that you would cultivate in me an appreciation of your goodness and a longing to worship you constantly.

THE GOOD FATHER

"And I will be a father to you,
and you shall be sons and daughters to me,"
says the Lord Almighty.
2 CORINTHIANS 6:18 ESV

We can easily confuse God's majesty with distance. We begin to think of him as someone who is out of touch with our daily lives—absent and uninterested. But the opposite is true!

God is a loving and kind father who takes interest in our deepest thoughts as a father does for his children. He loves us deeply and sensitively, as only a truly good father can. When we adjust our perception of God from far off to profoundly near, our intimacy with him can only deepen.

Thank you, God, that you are a good father. Thank you that you see me as your daughter and that you care deeply about me. Help me to see you as the father that you are, and not as the distant God that the world often portrays you to be.

GRACIOUS

Yet the Lord longs to be gracious to you;
therefore he will rise up to show you compassion.
For the Lord is a God of justice.
Blessed are all who wait for him!
   ISAIAH 30:18 NIV

We can become so overwhelmed by our own shame, troubles, or misconceptions that we miss out on the most simple and beautiful truth—our God greatly desires to show us grace. He doesn't long to show us his anger or his punishment. He doesn't rise up to show us his power and his terrible greatness; he rises up to show us compassion.

When we enter God's presence with this point of view, we are humbled by his love despite his justice—because the punishment we deserve has been outweighed by the grace he longs to give.

I am humbled by the power of your grace for me. Help me to wait for you and to always rely on your grace and your compassion more than my own strength and capacity for goodness.

November 12

UNDERSTAND AND ACCEPT

What we have received is not the spirit of the world, but the Spirit who is from God, so that we may understand what God has freely given us.

1 CORINTHIANS 2:12 NIV

The goodness of God toward us is so far beyond our human capacity for goodness that we struggle to understand it. Our difficulty in understanding God's gifts can ultimately lead to difficulty in our ability to accept them.

But at salvation, God puts his spirit within us—enabling us to understand his love, mercy, and grace. With the spirit of God in us, we can both comprehend and accept in full what the Father has given to us.

Heavenly Father, thank you for your great mercy, love, and goodness toward me. Thank you that through your spirit I can understand and accept all of your good gifts.

THE GOODNESS IN WAITING

The Lord is wonderfully good to those who wait for him, to those who seek for him. It is good both to hope and wait quietly for the salvation of the Lord.

LAMENTATIONS 3:25-26 TLB

Have you ever watched other people enjoy their "happily-ever-afters" while you sat wondering if yours would ever come? Sometimes it feels as though everyone else has their lives perfectly in order while your own is in some type of chaos.

Finding yourself waiting is challenging enough without watching everyone else rush ahead of you. But God promises goodness to those who are kept waiting. If you choose to seek the Lord as you wait, he will reveal himself to you in a sweeter way than you could have known otherwise.

Help me, God, to see waiting as a blessed opportunity to know your goodness. Teach me to wait quietly and with hope for you.

IN THE LIGHT

With You is the fountain of life;
In Your light we see light.
PSALM 36:9 NKJV

How would you explain color to a blind person? What is blue, and what makes it unique from red, purple, or green? In order to understand pink, you need to have experienced it.

It is the same with goodness, love, and light. In order to recognize it, we must know it. In order to know it, we must know the Father. He is the one true source of all light, of all that is good.

Abba, I want to live in the light! You are the source of its warmth; its life-giving power is from you. As the source of all that is good, you are all I need. Thank you, Lord, for your ever-flowing fountain. I drink in your goodness today, seeing evidence of your light all around me.

BEST DAY EVER

A single day in your courts
is better than a thousand anywhere else!
I would rather be a gatekeeper in the house of my God
than live the good life in the homes of the wicked.
PSALM 84:10 NLT ·

Remember the best day of your life. Would you trade nearly three years of your life for that precious memory, let's say living to 85 instead of 88? Now magnify the greatness of that wonderful day beyond your imagining; picture a day in God's presence. How many ordinary days would that be worth?

Answer this next question thoughtfully: would you rather be poor, yet surrounded by people full of love and integrity, or wealthy among those who compromise morality and goodness as a matter of course?

Lord, examine my heart. Am I living a life that reflects my desire for you? What would you have me change? Where would you have me go?

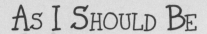

As I Should Be

There is surely a future hope for you,
and your hope will not be cut off.
PROVERBS 23:18 NIV

God made you. Carefully, intentionally, he made you. And he knew exactly what he was doing, and why. Even the desires of your heart are there on purpose: to lead the Father's plan for your life.

The next time you doubt your worth, remember these words. The next time your question your purpose, look to your passions. What wonderful things did he prepare in advance for you to do?

Lord, sometimes I doubt myself. All I see are my many flaws, and all I feel is the weight of my sin. Thank you for reminding me that to you, I am exactly as I should be. I am who and how you made me. Lead me, Father, to the good you'd have me do.

BURIED TALENTS

"Whoever has will be given more, and they will have an abundance. Whoever does not have, even what they have will be taken from them."

MATHEW 25:29 NIV

God, in his well-executed plan, endowed his children with talents. In Matthew 25:15, we get a small glimpse of his purpose in putting unique gifts within each of us. God alone decides how many talents he will entrust us with. These talents are graciously endowed to us and are not actually meant for our own benefit; they are intended to be a blessing to others.

Is the thought of exercising your talents so overwhelming in your already hectic schedule that you have chosen to bury it instead? Buried talents do nobody any good. Exercising your talent will actually become life giving to you.

Jesus, please push me forward, even when I push back. I pray for the grace to serve in the way that you equipped and created me to.

THORNS

In order to keep me from becoming conceited, I was given a thorn in my flesh... Three times I pleaded with the Lord to take it away from me.

2 CORINTHIANS 12:7-8 NIV

Would you like some great news today? Every child of God is profoundly imperfect. In addition to being imperfect, we all have besetting weaknesses. Many of these weaknesses can be managed and some, through the power of God, can actually be healed. But rest assured; weaknesses will not altogether go away. Once one is conquered, you will often find that another gets exposed. They are part of humanity.

What is your thorn? What area do you wrestle in continually? Paul, the great hero of our faith, also wrestled with a besetting weakness. God wants us to remain weak so that we can be strong in him. We are forced to remain in the place of humility, clinging to God for strength and comfort.

Thank you, God, for giving me thorns. Even though I don't like them, I know they are good for me. They keep me humble and trusting in you. Help me to cling to you for strength in every area of my life.

BLOOM WHERE YOU ARE PLANTED

"They are those who, hearing the word, hold it fast in an honest and good heart, and bear fruit with patience."
LUKE 8:15 ESV

Most of us want to make a significant mark somewhere in our lifetime. It's comforting to believe that the routine of our ordinary lives is merely preparation for the really big assignment that surely is just around the corner. You know, the lofty thing, the high calling, the noble assignment that undoubtedly is directly ahead.

Then one day in a moment of quiet, the Lord whispers, "This is it. What you are doing is what I've called you to do. Do your work, raise your kids, love your neighbor, serve people, seek me first, and everything in your heart you long for will be fulfilled. Be faithful right where I've put you. You don't need to accomplish great things for me. Just be."

Lord, I so long for significance. I want my life to matter. Help me to understand that it's not what I do for you that is important... it's whose I am and who I am. Help me to be faithful in the assignment you have given me right now.

STARTING OVER

Praise the LORD!
Oh, give thanks to the LORD, for He is good!
For His mercy endures forever.
PSALM 106:1 NKJV

Have you ever wished you could have a do-over? It would be so great to turn back the clock, reverse a decision, and do it differently. There is so much more wisdom in looking back! Yes, there are some things we can do over, like tweak the recipe or rip the seam, but most often, the important big decisions can't be changed.

Except when it comes to spiritual things. God tells us that we can start over every morning because his mercies will be there. Whatever went awry the day before, whatever mess we made from poor choices, we can begin the next day with a completely clean slate! There does not need to be any carryover of yesterday's mistakes. Our part in the transaction may require repentance of sin or forgiving someone, perhaps even ourselves. Bathed in his mercies, we can begin each day squeaky clean!

LORD, I am so grateful that your love and your mercies never end. You extend them to me brand new every morning! Great is your faithfulness!

FOUND DELIGHTFUL

Let those who delight in my righteousness
shout for joy and be glad
and say evermore,
"Great is the Lord,
who delights in the welfare of his servant!"
PSALM 35:27 ESV

Despite this season of thanksgiving, it can be a struggle to find delight. If the holiday spirit isn't quite abundant, take delight in God's righteousness. *Shout for joy and be glad!* And hold fast to the promise of his delight in you. His delight isn't circumstantial.

Regardless of your situation today, God finds you delightful. It isn't a patronizing delight, like an adult chuckling while a toddler throws a temper tantrum; rather, he sees right past whatever emotion we are expressing to the depths of who he knows us to be.

God, you see all of me and still find me delightful. You promise that my past triumphs and current struggles all lead to a future of strength in you. I am humbled to be found delightful by you, and desire to shout for joy and be glad, delighting in you all the more!

STRONGHOLD

The LORD is good,
A stronghold in the day of trouble;
And He knows those who trust in Him.
NAHUM 1:7 NKJV

God isn't only with us when our faith comes easy and our praise is unrestrained. Even in the day of trouble, God knows intimately those who trust him, and he is a stronghold for them.

Not only in catastrophe, but even in our moments of hidden weakness, God is our strength and our refuge. We can trust him and know that he is always good.

Thank you, Lord, that you are a source of strength for me even in my weakest moments. You remember my trust in you when I feel close to losing my faith. You do not forget me, and you are more than enough for me. You take my darkest hour and bring the light of your countenance to me.

WORTHY

"You are worthy, O Lord,
To receive glory and honor and power;
For You created all things,
And by Your will they exist and were created."
REVELATION 4:11 NKJV

Worship is our natural response to the goodness of God. It's not simply an emotional reaction—worship is also the act of offering back to God the glory that he rightly deserves. When we stop to think about God's power, majesty, and creativity, we cannot help but glorify him because he is so worthy of the highest form of honor.

By glorifying God in our daily lives, those around us will take notice and some will ultimately be led to join us in praising him.

God help me to praise you in the way that you are worthy of. Help me to respond to you with honor, appreciation, and worship. I want to look for you in everything, so I can give praise back to you for all you've done.

FATHER KNOWS BEST

We are confident that he hears whenever we ask for anything that pleases him. And since we know he hears us when we make our requests, we also know that he will give us what we ask for.

1 JOHN 5:14-15 NLT

Our prayers are not offered up to a silent heaven. When we pray, we are heard by a God who cares deeply about what we bring before him. By understanding the depth of his interest we gain confidence to approach him boldly in prayer.

God is a good Father who will not be swayed into giving us anything that is not to our benefit. We can present our requests to God freely, knowing that if what we ask for is not what is best for our lives, then it will not be given to us.

Thank you, God, that you answer my prayers in accordance with your perfect will. Help me to trust that you know exactly what is best for me.

STORED GOODNESS

How abundant are the good things
that you have stored up for those who fear you,
that you bestow in the sight of all,
on those who take refuge in you.

PSALM 31:19 NIV

David, who enjoyed a great friendship with God, makes many wonderfully startling claims about God. God is storing up goodness! What exactly is that goodness? Is it safety and security? Is it peace in trials? Is it a quiet heart in the middle of a storm? Is it joy in the midst of mourning? Yes, it would seem that his goodness could be all of these and much more.

There is so much goodness that God actually has to store it, so he doesn't drench us in it all at once. But there is a caveat. The goodness referenced in this passage is reserved for a special group of people—those who fear God. It is for those who humbly come to him because he is the King and they are not. Rest assured, God will reward you more than your wildest dreams for loving him like that.

Help me, Jesus, to trust in God's goodness like you did when you were on the earth. Thank you that you see my faith even when it's weak and you store up goodness for me.

WATER OF LIFE

"Whoever drinks of the water that I shall give him will never thirst. But the water that I shall give him will become in him a fountain of water springing up into everlasting life."

JOHN 4:14 NKJV

Sometimes, we need "extra." Our spiritual requirements are never met by earthly experiences. When these experiences occlude our spiritual opportunities, we leave off from them, thirsting. Life as expected derails—whether from internal failures or external events—and this creates great inner struggle. The verve inside us may dwindle in the face of such difficult challenges. Where will we get joy and strength to continue?

Jesus says he brings us abundant life *wherever* the enemy has tried to steal, kill, or destroy. He is just that faithful. His living water is an endless fountain. We reach up to him, relying upon him to fill us with this eternal life.

Jesus, I praise you. Thank you for being good to me and loving me. Please pour your "extra" into my thirsty soul as I pour your holy Word into my life. Envelope me in your presence, and train me to stand in you, as a relentless and immoveable child of your joy.

FALSE EXPECTATIONS

This is how we know what love is: Jesus Christ laid down his life for us. And we ought to lay down our lives for our brothers and sisters.

1 JOHN 3:16 NIV

Part of laying down one's life rests in relinquishing inappropriate expectations. When the highlight reel of your mind doesn't match your life, you hand that reel to Jesus. He returns to you belonging and peace. These two blessings hinge upon your identity in him, not upon your attempts to achieve.

God places his desires within the hearts of his holy ones. When they are ignited, these desires produce good things: creativity, productivity, and charity toward others. You are not a failure. You are a possibility—*God's possibility*—opening up in the light of Jesus like a flower in sunshine, coming into its full bloom.

Thank you, God, that my life is not a mistake but a unique expression of your nature. Help me to be myself and live according to who I am, not according to expectations that create an ill-fitting yoke.

LEVELING UP

Trust in the LORD with all your heart,
and do not lean on your own understanding.
In all your ways acknowledge him,
and he will make straight your paths.

PROVERBS 3:5-6 ESV

As we learn to walk in surrender to the Holy Spirit, our heavenly Father beckons us to a higher level of intimacy with him. In order to do this, we must become vulnerable and get real with him. We must continually trust him more than our experiences or reasoning.

When we trust God without boundaries, we find him more reliable than anyone else. We are wrapped in his love—the safest place we could find ourselves. Constantly leaning our hearts toward him, and choosing what he would, we receive his comfort and guidance, and our paths become straight.

Heavenly Father, I come to you and ask you to help me trust you, knowing that you have the best in store for me. Have your way with me. I release control, and I trust in you. You are for me, not against me. I love you.

GUIDED

I will lead the blind
by a road they do not know,
by paths they have not known
I will guide them.
I will turn the darkness before them into light,
the rough places into level ground.
These are the things I will do,
and I will not forsake them.

ISAIAH 42:16 NRSV

When you feel that you have lost your way, and your feet can't feel the path beneath you, God promises that he will lead you forward. Even if you can't see what lies ahead, and though the road feels rocky and unsure, God will guide you. The path that seemed impassable will become smooth and the way that seemed impossible will become straightforward.

God promises that he will do this for you and more—because he loves you and his is a love that never fails or forsakes.

Thank you for your promise to guide me no matter how impossible the way seems.

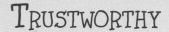

TRUSTWORTHY

For the word of the LORD holds true,
and we can trust everything he does.
>   PSALM 33:4 NLT

All of us have experienced our fair share of hurt. We've been jaded by failed dreams, broken relationships, and empty promises. No matter how hurt or worn down we may feel, we can always trust God with our hearts. He will never lie to us, manipulate us, or let us down. He will never go back on his word to us, abandon us, or stop loving us.

The Lord is always true to his Word. Who he has been throughout the ages is who he remains today. The God we read about in Scripture— who never forgot his covenants and loved irrevocably—is the same God who holds our hearts today.

Thank you, Lord, that in a world where trust is broken daily, I can always trust you perfectly. Please heal my heart from the hurt I've experienced so that I can love you more deeply.

DECEMBER

I will meditate on your majestic, glorious splendor
and your wonderful miracles.
Your awe-inspiring deeds will be on every tongue;
I will proclaim your greatness.
Everyone will share the story of
your wonderful goodness;
they will sing with joy about
your righteousness.

PSALM 145:5-7 NLT

ROCKS DON'T CHANGE

Trust in the LORD forever,
for the LORD, the LORD himself, is the Rock eternal.
ISAIAH 26:4 NIV

When people talk about the most dependable person they know, they may describe that person as being their rock. These people represent a constant in our lives; the advice they give today is the same advice they'll give in twenty years. Their principles—and their love—are unwavering.

A rock placed in a box for decades will look exactly the same on the day it's rediscovered. Rocks don't change.

Lord, you are the rock eternal. I trust you with my life, Father, because I know your commitment to me is unwavering. I am safe with you. You want what you have always wanted; you are who you have always been. You are constant. You are good. You are love itself.

HIS PURPOSE FOR YOU

The LORD will fulfill his purpose for me;
your steadfast love, O LORD, endures forever.
Do not forsake the works of your hands.
    PSALM 138:8 ESV

Did you know God is more intent on fulfilling his purpose for your life than you are? He is fully aware you are the weaker vessel in your relationship with him. While we might have zeal and passion, we naturally grow weak, lazy, or idle. This can be discouraging to us, but God is not easily discouraged. After all, he is our Maker and knows exactly how frail we are.

God can fulfill his purpose for you because his love will endure over you forever. It is not a weak love. You are the precious work of his hands.

God, help me trust you and partner with you in fulfilling your purpose for my life. Thank you that you made me with a purpose and that I am not a mistake.

JUST BECAUSE

Honor the LORD for the glory of his name.
Worship the LORD in the splendor of his holiness.
PSALM 29:2 NLT

It isn't your birthday, but there's a gift on the counter with your name on it. You haven't done anything particularly special lately, but a card arrives in the mail to let you know you are loved—just because. It feels wonderful. It feels even better when you are on the giving end.

When is the last time you worshipped God just for being God? He loves to receive spontaneous gifts of love, honor, and praise just as much as we do.

Lord, above all other names, I worship yours. I meditate on your holiness, your perfection, and it brings me to my knees. I love you, God, for who you are and I thank you for who you are helping me to become.

An Incomprehensible Gift

When people work, their wages are not a gift, but something they have earned. But people are counted as righteous, not because of their work, but because of their faith in God who forgives sinners.

ROMANS 4:4-5 NLT

No matter how much a person loved their job, if their employer stopped paying them, they'd eventually stop working. Conversely, if the employee stopped working, the employer would inevitably stop signing paychecks. In an employment agreement, both parties have to honor their part for it to work.

This is what makes our relationship—our mutual agreement—with Jesus so astonishing. His part of the agreement was death on a cross to ensure our salvation. Our part is belief.

Lord Jesus, I will never deserve your sacrifice. No matter how hard I work, I will never even the scale. Today, I thank you for the incomprehensible gift of my salvation.

TELL YOUR STORY

Let the redeemed of the LORD tell their story—
those he redeemed from the hand of the foe.
PSALM 107:2 NIV

What's your story? Whether it's so complex you barely know where to begin, or you think it's too insignificant to tell, be assured that it matters.

From the beginning, God had you in mind. He planned you out to the tiniest detail. He has loved you forever. The way in which you discovered this beautiful truth, or the way it is currently unfolding, is of great significance. Begin telling it to yourself, and be ready to share it when the time comes.

Lord, when I consider your story, mine seems so small. That you chose me to be a part of it is too wonderful to comprehend. Thank you for my story, Father. May I learn to see it as you do: significant, beautiful, and worthy.

Now I Am Found!

"Rejoice with me; I have found my lost sheep."
LUKE 15:6 NIV

How pleasing it is to find something that we thought we had lost!
We rejoice in the small victories of finding a lost receipt, pair of
sunglasses, or even that matching sock! There is something in our
created nature that tells us loss is something to be grieved and
discovery is to be celebrated!

The parable of the lost sheep makes it abundantly clear that Jesus
celebrates every life that is found in him. The heavens celebrate your
salvation, and though you are one of many, Jesus has gone out of the
way to find *you*. Such is his love for his own.

Jesus, I thank you for being my shepherd. I thank you for
seeking me out and saving me. I thank you that you rejoice
in my salvation. Help me to know my significance in you and
to share in your delight each time I hear of the salvation of
others.

OPENED, LIFTED, AND LOVED

The LORD opens the eyes of the blind;
The LORD raises up those who are bowed down;
The LORD loves the righteous.
PSALM 146:8 NASB

Our God loves to restore life to his creation. When Jesus came to earth, he healed many physical needs. Greater than physical healing, Jesus came to restore our spiritual brokenness. He opened eyes to the truth, ministered to the poor in spirit, and restored believers to righteousness.

How blessed you are. He has opened your eyes, he will always lift you up in times of trouble, and he loves you because you have chosen the path of righteousness. Let the God of encouragement and restoration be your strength today.

God, you have opened my eyes to the truth; you have forgiven my sin, and you love me. Some days I have fallen harder than others, and today I need you to once again bring restoration to my body and soul. Thank you for picking me up and encouraging me on the path of righteousness.

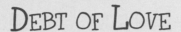

DEBT OF LOVE

Let no debt remain outstanding, except the continuing debt
to love one another, for whoever loves others has fulfilled the
law.

ROMANS 13:8 NIV

When a bill arrives in the mail, we are reminded that we owe money
in return for something that has been done for us. If we leave it
for too long, it can cause anxiety and even resentment on both
sides. This is one reason the Scripture reminds us not to leave a debt
outstanding.

However, the Bible instructs us to treat love as debt, in the sense that
we should continually be compelled to love one another and to give
love even if it has not been earned! This is the extreme love that God
has shown us. Let his unending and unconditional love for you be the
reminder letter that you need to spur you on to love others in the
same way.

Jesus, you continue to amaze me with the love that you have
for me. I know that I don't need to earn your love and that you
will never give up on me. Remind me, Holy Spirit, to continue
to love others in this way.

A Patient Promise

The Lord is not slow about His promise, as some count slowness, but is patient toward you, not wishing for any to perish but for all to come to repentance.

2 PETER 3:9 NASB

Jesus will return one day—he promised he would! Until then, however, we live in the "in-between." The kingdom has come, but not in its fullness, and we await the time when the earth and everything in it will be restored.

Jesus' return can seem slow to those of us who are waiting, but if we understand the love that Jesus has for humanity, we can understand, in part, his timing for waiting for others to reach repentance. Praise Jesus for his love, and be patient in his promise. He will return!

Jesus, I don't fully understand your way and why some of the promises that I read about in your Word have not been fulfilled. Give me a holy patience, one that understands your heart for the world. Grant me that same heart for those who don't know you yet. Lead us all to repentance.

CONVINCED OF LOVE

I am convinced that neither death, nor life, nor angels, nor rulers, nor things present, nor things to come, nor powers, nor height, nor depth, nor anything else in all creation, will be able to separate us from the love of God in Christ Jesus our Lord.

ROMANS 8:38-39 NRSV

Our relationship with Jesus Christ is eternal. You may have just begun this journey with him, or have been a friend of God for all of your life. Whatever your life story, you are covered by his grace and can never be separated from his love.

Jesus Christ is all about love for his people. He humbled himself and took on human form for you. He suffered rejection for you. He took himself to the cross and died for you. Nothing would have stopped his love for you. His love will surround you in the highest height and the deepest depth. Be convinced that nothing will separate you from the love you have found in Jesus.

Jesus, thank you for everything you have endured for me. Thank you for showing me love by sacrificing your life for me. I acknowledge that I may never fully understand the love that you have for me, but I am convinced that nothing will separate me from your love.

RETURNED LOVE

I love those who love me,
and those who seek me find me.
PROVERBS 8:17 NIV

With God, we never have to worry about being the one who bestows unrequited love. We always know, with absolute certainty, that our love—no matter how passionate—is even more passionately returned. God loves those who love him; he wants to be sought by you. But even more than that, he longs to be found by you.

Don't think that when you cry out to him you're speaking to thin air. He hears you and loves you. He gives himself to you. Continue in your love for him. Continue in your pursuit of him. He will give himself to you with even greater abandon than you can imagine.

Jesus, thank you for loving me perfectly. Thank you for giving yourself to me fully. Thank you that you have made a way for me to enter your glory and to be loved by you forever.

HIS RICHES

This same God who takes care of me will supply all your
needs from his glorious riches, which have been given to
us in Christ Jesus.

PHILIPPIANS 4:19 NLT

The Lord's riches are found in his goodness, his grace, and his
sovereignty as king over all. God is always able to provide for all of
our needs. Sometimes we may feel as though we are not worthy to
receive from the Lord. Sometimes we find it hard to trust and we
worry about our needs.

The good news of Jesus Christ is that he has given us access to the
throne of God. You are a child of the king and he offers his riches to
you. All you need to do is love him, ask him, and trust in his goodness.
His promise is to take care of you.

Almighty God, you are sovereign and good. Thank you that
you want to take care of me. There are things that I feel I need
right now and I submit them to you. I pray you would take the
burden from me as I continue to trust you each and every day.

December 13

TRUE LOVE

"All people will know that you are my followers if you love each other."

JOHN 13:35 NCV

We are commanded to love one another. But, love isn't easy. There are parts of every human relationship that are broken. Love is often about repair. You love each other past the difficulty and in spite of the inconvenience. True love is patient enough to rise above challenges and seek solutions. True love doesn't look to satisfy itself; true love gives.

When God defined love, he did it through sacrifice, demonstrating that there is no room for selfishness in love.

God, I want to be known as your follower. Teach me to love like you so I can demonstrate your love to those around me. Give me the strength required to be selfless in my love and devoted in my relationships.

TOTALLY COMMITTED

The LORD is faithful; he will strengthen you
and guard you from the evil one.

2 THESSALONIANS 3:3 NLT

Faithful friends never betray you. A faithful dog sticks close to your side. A faithful spouse has eyes only for you.

The Lord is faithful. Allow this incredible truth to strengthen and sustain you as you face whatever the enemy has planned today. God will never betray you; the creator of the universe never leaves your side; Jesus will never choose another over you.

Lord, who am I that you are unwavering in your commitment to me? My own faithfulness wavers from day to day. I see things I want; I face issues I'd rather not, and sin lures me away from you. Today, God, I am totally committed to you. I marvel anew at your love and draw my strength from the wellspring of your faithfulness.

ABIDING LOVE

Satisfy us in the morning with your unfailing love,
that we may sing for joy and be glad all our days.
PSALM 90:14 NIV

Think of brand-new love, where the newness and the enthusiasm are almost overwhelming. Whether a romance, a new pet, or even a new fitness plan, that feeling may or may not take root.

Let us make sure we are rooted in our relationship with Jesus. Has the joy of discovering him given way to the deeper joy of knowing him and walking with him each day?

Lord, my heart overflows with thankfulness as I consider all you've done for me. Strengthen my faith, Jesus, as I live my life in your deep, abiding strength and love. I sink my roots down right here, into my love for you.

STEADFAST LOVE

As high as the heavens are above the earth,
so great is his steadfast love toward those who fear him.
PSALM 103:11 ESV

Let's take a moment to contemplate steadfast love. Steadfast love is steady. It doesn't get offended easily. It can weather incredible relational strain. It can handle faithlessness. It won't quit even when the recipient's love has grown cold.

This is steadfast love. And this is how God describes his love toward his children. He promises fidelity and faithful love even when you aren't faithful to him. If you run from him, upon your repentance he stands ready to accept you and pour more of his steadfast love upon you. He won't charge you for it or remind you of your weakness. He will simply strengthen you.

Father, thank you that you are different than I am. Thank you that your love is pure and steadfast. Help me to believe and trust you for that today.

YOUR EYES WILL SEE

Your eyes will see the King in His beauty;
They will behold a far-distant land.
ISAIAH 33:17 NASB

On the difficult days when our faith is weak, our tears flow freely, and our hearts are discouraged, we wish just to see God. We think that if we could look into his eyes, have the chance to ask him our deepest questions—and hear them answered—then we could continue on.

Beloved, the reality of heaven is closer than we can imagine. We will see our King, in all his greatness and his beauty. We will look upon that distant land of heaven. We will one day dwell there in peace: with every question answered and every tear dried.

Thank you, God, that you have promised heaven to me through my belief in your Son. Thank you that I will see your face one day and walk with you in your kingdom. When the days are hard, help me to remember that in just a little while all will be well and I will be with you.

UNHINDERED

Because of Christ and our faith in him, we can now come boldly and confidently into God's presence.
EPHESIANS 3:12 NLT

Our salvation awards us the great privilege of being able to approach God unhindered. With sin no longer dividing us from his holy presence, we are free to bare our souls to God as his beloved sons and daughters.

As bold and confident lovers of God, there is nothing we cannot share with him—and he with us. Fear and shame have no place in this kind of excellent love.

I love you, Lord. I praise you that you made a way for me to love you unhindered. I don't want my fear and my shame to interrupt our relationship—so I ask you to take it from me. Show me what it means to be a bold and confident child of yours.

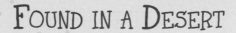

FOUND IN A DESERT

He found them in a desert,
a windy, empty land.
He surrounded them and brought them up,
guarding them as those he loved very much.

DEUTERONOMY 32:10 NCV

Do you ever go through seasons in your life where you just feel dark? Perhaps directionless or uninspired? In a metaphorical wilderness where you can't get a glimpse of any vision or even hope, God can find you. Even in the deserts of your own heart where you can't muster the strength to reach out to him, he can and will meet you.

Wait for the Lord, even in your emptiness; wait for him and he will come for you.

Thank you, Father, that you are near to me even when my heart is broken and my strength has failed. Thank you that you find me in my wilderness and you will restore me to joy.

COLLECTED TEARS

You have seen me tossing and turning through the night. You have collected all my tears and preserved them in your bottle! You have recorded every one in your book.

PSALM 56:8 TLB

Our grief is near to God's heart. He longs to console us: to stroke our hair, wipe our tears, and whisper comfort. He counts the nights we toss and turn; he collects our tears. God isn't absent in our sorrow, rather the opposite—he is closer than ever.

Don't be afraid to come to God with your grief. Share with him the deepest feelings in your heart without holding back. In his presence you will find comfort, hope, compassion, and more love than you could imagine.

Thank you, Jesus, for holding me in my sadness. I need your strength even more in my grief. Please be near to me and comfort me in your presence.

PEACE IN JESUS: THE ETERNAL GIFT

"Give glory to God in heaven, and on earth let there be peace among the people who please God."
LUKE 2:14 NCV

Christmas trees might be secular decorations, but they invoke, in Christians, thoughts of a more precious tree: the cross. Jesus came to us on Christmas day for the purpose of bringing peace to his people through the cross of Calvary.

Christ's mission was to redeem us from every thought, word, or action that didn't match up to our God-likeness. He destroyed our sins and silenced our enemy, permanently, on the cross. He empowered us for victory. Each of us carries his glory as a child of the Most High God. This is a Christmas gift for each of us to open every day.

Holy Father, thank you for this gift. Please toss out the broken ornaments of my life, and remake me according to your glory. Give me peace. I affirm you as my Lord, and I'll take orders from you. Thank you for loving me so tenderly. I love you, too.

THE LOVE-JOY LIFE

"As the Father has loved me, so have I loved you. Abide in my love. If you keep my commandments, you will abide in my love, just as I have kept my Father's commandments and abide in his love. These things I have spoken to you, that my joy may be in you, and that your joy may be full."

JOHN 15:9-11 ESV

Joy comes into our lives through actions of obedience. Moreover, we may obey God for the sake of righteousness, but God rewards us for it in baptizing us in his love! As we abide in this love, we become vessels of joy, spilling onto dry places in the world around us. That joy will consume us, becoming a hallmark of his righteousness.

Strength and courage rise in the context of God's joy. We pursue and choose his ways, gaining fortitude to overcome, and we begin to live the supernatural life. In following the faithful one who overcame the world, we become like him, and we overcome as well.

Thank you, Lord, for hearing my cry for mercy. You are my strength and shield. Thank you for loving me. Help me to abide in your love.

CHARITY

If anyone has material possessions and sees a brother or sister in need but has no pity on them, how can the love of God be in that person? Dear children, let us not love with words or speech but with actions and in truth.

1 JOHN 3:17-18 NIV

The Christmas season is filled with opportunities to give. More so than during any other time of the year, charities offer venues for community service and vehicles for giving to others. In response, we drop money into buckets, tuck gifts under angel trees, and say extra prayers for those in need. In addition, we may find ourselves watering flowers for traveling neighbors or hosting a dinner party for those without family. Being a soft spot for those bruised souls in our path is a mark of discipleship.

Nobody wants to be alone or hungry on Christmas. Nobody wants to give their kids regretful hugs instead of gifts, shelter, or homemade food. In a time of hope and gladness, your active love reaches beyond the circumstances of the afflicted.

God, may my hands and my supply bless the hearts of those who are in need this season. I ask you to give of yourself through me. Help me to be a willing vessel of your blessing to those who so desperately need it.

HE TEACHES ME ACCEPTANCE

"I have brought you glory on earth by finishing the work you gave me to do."
JOHN 17:4 NIV

As we walk in love as faithful children, we will see fruit develop from what we do. We bring life and joy, truth and gentleness. We bring our gifts and ambitions. Often, this is met with delight and gratitude. Other times, people don't understand our intentions. Still other times, we sow our gifts faithfully, and never see good come of it. Oftentimes, it is because the gifts God gives us are a portion of a legacy that cannot be recognized in a generation. You may be feeding the poor, heartbroken that there is not enough water. You may be clothing the naked, weeping that their bills won't be paid this month.

The point is this: you are being faithful. God is proud of you. And though the world around you may not understand what you are doing, and though you may not understand the world around you, Jesus has everything handled. He is making beautiful things in and with you. That is enough. Just walk with him in faith.

God, there is so much of the world I don't understand. Some of it I don't want to know. Make me bold to trust you and to know that everything will be okay as I rest in you and walk in life.

SEEK, THEN BOLDLY PROCLAIM!

They hurried off and found Mary and Joseph, and the baby, who was lying in the manger. When they had seen him, they spread the word concerning what had been told them about this child, and all who heard it were amazed at what the shepherds said to them.

LUKE 2:16-18 NIV

When the shepherds were told about Jesus, they didn't pencil him into their schedules; they ran to him! They ran as fast as their feet could carry them. Who watched over the sheep? Who knows! But in that moment, they knew the importance of the Lord's advent, and they rushed in to Bethlehem, and into his barn stall, to see him. Once they rushed to him, and experienced him, they rushed to tell of him. God didn't choose earthly leaders to spread the word. He chose messengers who would faithfully carry the good news.

Who is this Lord of ours, that fishermen and ranch hands spread his good news? Hallelujah! Christ has come! Tell your friends! Tell your neighbors! Tell everyone you meet: Jesus is the Lord, and he has come in the flesh! Hallelujah!

Lord, thank you for coming to exchange beauty for ashes, joy for mourning, and praise for heaviness. I sing to the world with all my soul, "Glory to God in the highest heaven!"

HE DELIGHTS IN YOU

The LORD directs the steps of the godly.
He delights in every detail of their lives.
Though they stumble, they will never fall,
for the LORD holds them by the hand.

PSALM 37:23-24 NLT

Jesus lives in you by choice. He has saved you quite capably. He is excited merely by being with you. Jesus doesn't need you to earn his gladness. He promises to calm your fears in his love. He is so happy that you exist that the very joy of it causes him to burst forth into singing as he dances and twirls about you.

You are encompassed and filled with God's no-holds-barred, unabashed delight... in you.

Thank you, Jesus, that you are the maker and redeemer of my soul. Thank you for your unabashed joy toward me and your delight in me. I am in awe of your goodness.

DRESSED FOR THE WEATHER

Put on the new self, created to be like God in true
righteousness and holiness.
EPHESIANS 4:24 NIV

You have such a beautiful future ahead of you! What a blessing it is
that you will affect people by just being you: lovely, holy, and loved
of God. Because you are a child of God, your home isn't here. It's in
heaven, where spiritual weather is always fine. If you go out into
an earthly storm, you change your inward clothes to meet earthly
challenges before you.

Earth isn't your home turf; life here is laden with storms. Fortunately,
Christ has given you ample covering for the weather. Put on the new
man to overcome with Christ. He has offered it to you, and he finds it
precious that you wear the clothing he provides you.

Jesus, thank you for empowering me to put on the new man
and discard the old. Thank you for overcoming the world
and offering for me to dwell safely in your light's protective
warmth. I will walk in faith as the storms of life blow around
me.

UNDESERVED GIFTS

David asked, "Is there anyone still left of the house of Saul to whom I can show kindness for Jonathan's sake?"

2 SAMUEL 9:1 NIV

In the story of David, we meet an infirmed grandchild of Saul named Mephibosheth. Because of Saul's cruelty to David, Mephibosheth would have been an unlikely candidate for David's favor. David had the heart of God, though. For the sake of his friend, Jonathan, David granted Mephibosheth a regular seat at his table as well as his grandfather's entire estate and the servants he needed. David extended luxurious favor upon one who could not possibly benefit him, and who did not think himself a friend.

It is true: God is quizzically kind and compassionate to all people, regardless of how they stand with him. Although you may feel you have let God down, or you have little to offer, Jesus invites you to his feast table every day. He welcomes you to stay in his presence so you will enjoy the lavish care he continually gives you.

Lord, thank you for loving me so well. Please show me your grace and mercy, and help me to extend it, as I bubble over in your goodness. Make me wise in all things, Father.

ETERNALLY BLESSED

How blessed is the man who fears the LORD,
Who greatly delights in His commandments.
PSALM 112:1 NASB

Blessings from God are gifts given as a result of his grace toward
us. We can grow in God's graces just as we grow in the graces of
the people around us. When we revere him and abide in his love, we
naturally obey him from the heart. As our hearts knit together with
God's, this grace improves.

The Lord keeps you steadfast, secure, and ultimately triumphant as
you fear and obey him.

Lord, please train my heart to fear and honor you in everything I
do. I want to know your intimate and sovereign presence, to cling
to you in it, and to become a rich and timeless blessing to you
and the people you touch through me.

ORIGIN OF STRENGTH

"People do not live by bread alone, but by every word that comes from the mouth of God."

MATTHEW 4:4 NLT

When Jesus was tempted by the devil, he had been in the wilderness fasting for forty days and forty nights. He wasn't consuming any calories during that time. Instead, he was giving all his energy to communing with the Father and being strengthened by their relationship. At the end of that time, Satan came to tempt him. Jesus withstood authentic temptation and never gave in.

It's interesting how God prepared Jesus for this trial. He didn't have him attend a conference, read a self-help book, or have a healing service. Instead, he led his son to be physically weaker so he could lean fully on the Father and not his own strength. Jesus had been on a 40-day diet of love, affirmation, and encouragement from his Father. He wasn't weakened by his lack of food. In fact, he made it clear that food alone wasn't what made a child of God strong. Perhaps that's one of the greatest gifts in fasting—we are able to see that it isn't food that sustains us but God's power in us.

Father, thank you that we don't live on bread alone. Help us eat what we need to be strong in you: every Word that comes from your mouth.

LOAD OF ANXIETY

Always be full of joy in the Lord; I say it again, rejoice! Let everyone see that you are unselfish and considerate in all you do. Remember that the Lord is coming soon. Don't worry about anything; instead, pray about everything; tell God your needs, and don't forget to thank him for his answers.

PHILIPPIANS 4:4-6 TLB

Carrying anxiety is like over-packing a car for a trip. Gas mileage suffers, companions have a hard time joining you, and blocked vision endangers your car and others on the road. Clearly, you need to unpack anxiety in order to free yourself for a better journey. So, what is the key to shaking anxiety from your life? Rejoice in God, and gratefully request his help with your encumbrances.

Fortunately, joy in the Lord is available in all circumstances. It's that jug of lemonade in your fridge which readily fills your cup. Rejoicing produces refreshment. Your problems become manageable because Jesus is invited into all areas of your life. He is your accompanying reality—anxiety can no longer take that seat.

I rejoice in you, Lord! All of my being praises you! You are good; you are kind. You constantly walk with me. I praise you, and I know you are sovereign over my circumstances. They will pass, but you will always be with me. Come and still my heart.